THE
HOME
BREWER'S
HANDBOOK

BY DON GEARY

TAB BOOKS Inc.
BLUE RIDGE SUMMIT, PA. 17214

FIRST EDITION

FIRST PRINTING

Printed in the United States of America

Library of Congress Cataloging in Publication Data

Geary, Don.
    The home brewer's handbook.

    Includes index.
    1. Brewing—Amateurs' manuals.   I. Title.
TP570.G43   1983   641.8'73   82-5928
ISBN 0-8306-2461-9
ISBN 0-8306-1461-3 (pbk.)

Contents

Other TAB books by the author:

Introduction

I am often asked why I brew my own beer when I can buy a six-pack almost anywhere in the country for about $2. Part of the reason is that I can brew 5-gallons of good tasting beer for under $10 or about $1.10 per six-pack. Because we seem to consume more than the average family, this adds up to a considerable saving over the course of a year.

Another and possibly more important reason for having my own brewery is that I know what is in my beer. This is not often the case with commercially made beers. You surely have heard the claims about beechwood aging and old-world brewing methods, but American brewers are not required to list ingredients used on the label.

When you pop the top of your favorite brew, there might be any of 59 chemicals or other additives inside the can. Each one is permitted by law. The rich head that forms as you pour the beer into a glass may be the result of a squirt of propylene glycol alginate or gum arabic rather than fine hops and malt. The beer may be clear due to some proteases, and the golden color may come from caramel or even coal tar.

In Germany only water, malt, yeast, hops, and malt adjuncts (corn and rice, for example) are allowed in the brewing process. If you are sipping beer in America, you may be swallowing, in addition to those additives just mentioned, adipic acid, ethyl maltol, malic acid, octanal, potassium metabisulfite, sodium metabisulfite, grapefruit oil, lemon oil, tartaric acid, and possibly dozens of other additives.

These additives might be fine if we could always be sure of them and their possible side effects, but we don't know what is being used or the potential danger to us as beer drinkers. Cobalt sulfate, used at one time by commercial brewers to form a foaming, long lasting head, is now outlawed.

Anyone can brew good tasting beer at home. The cost of basic ingredients and equipment is less than $20. You can brew 5-gallons of great tasting beer for about $10. It will be ready to drink in two weeks. If you allow the beer to age for six weeks, though, the beer will be even better.

On 1 February 1979 Congress passed the Cranston bill. It permits the brewing of up to 100 gallons of beer per year in a one-adult household and up to 200 gallons of beer per year in households with two or more persons older than 18. There is no federal tax or permit required with these limitations.

Because state laws vary widely, there may be special regulations for you. Check with your state and county tax collection agencies; Bureau of Alcohol, Tobacco, and Firearms; and your local county clerk's office. Check your Yellow Pages for local listings.

All the information necessary to brew quality beers, ales, and stouts is given in this book. In addition to a basic brewing recipe, more advanced brewing techniques also are given. In a matter of months you should be able to brew beer that is better tasting and possibly better for you than any beer you can buy in this country.

Let schoolmasters puzzle their brains
with grammar and nonsense and learning
Good liquor I stoutly maintain
gives genius a better discerning

—Goldsmith

Beer and Its Origins

Beer seems to predate all written history. We do know, however, that the Egyptians and Romans brewed beer, so it has been around for at least 6000 years.

In western Europe ales have been brewed from grain since before written history. During the Dark Ages monasteries were in the forefront of developments in the basic brewing process. A brewmaster monk often was in charge of providing the household with a steady supply of brew throughout the year. In addition to something that resembles today's ales, fruits, berries, and flowers were also used to produce concoctions and potions.

Louis Pasteur, the father of *pasteurization*, also had a hand in beer making. Pasteur discovered that pasteurization—bringing beer to a specific temperature—has a stabilizing effect on it. It will have a longer shelf life. Pasteurization has a damaging effect on beer's taste. Most countries with a beer drinking population—Germany, Great Britain, etc.—do not pasteurize beer unless it is for export. The brewers of the United States commonly pasteurize all bottles and cans of beer, but not necessarily "keg" types of beer. The beer you brew at home will have a different taste from that which you buy at the local grocery store. If you are drinking liter mugs of beer in Munich, you will taste a beer that is truly more natural because it has not been pasteurized.

The home brewer can learn much from the western Europeans, particularly the Germans. Neither draft nor bottled beer is pasteurized in Germany. As mentioned in the Introduction, only five basic ingredients are allowed in German beer: water, hops, yeast, malt, and malt adjuncts (Fig. 1-1). American commercial brewers may use many other chemicals in beer and are not required to list them on the packaging.

German brewmasters, along with Dutch and English brewers, have helped to popularize pilsner beers in the United States.

Fig. 1-1. Only five ingredients are required for brewing great tasting beer.

If your main aim in home brewing is to derive quick, cheap, and as potent as possible suds, you can do this very easily. When taste is a consideration, however, you are faced with several important decisions, each of which can affect how the final brew turns out.

AMERICAN BEERS

You have probably sampled many local and national beers. A knowledge of different beer tastes is a sound basis for determining the drinkability of any beer.

If you live in the eastern United States, you generally have a wider selection of commercial beers at your disposal. That is in addition to the major brewery offerings of Budweiser, Miller High Life, Lowenbrau, etc. Easterners have Genesee, Schaefer, Rhinegold, Rolling Rock, Utica Club, and a few others. Imported beers from Canada—Schooner, Moose Head Ale, and Molson—and Europe—notably Heineken, Becks, and Dinkelacker—are available.

Westerners drink the most beer in the United States. Some special beers worth trying include Rainer Ale, Coors (one of the few canned and bottled beers that is not pasteurized), George Killian's Red Ale (also Coors), Olympia, Lone Star (Olympia Brewing Company), and Anchor Steam Beer.

All American beers currently offered are highly carbonated, lightly hopped, pale lager beers made by the same process. In the nineteenth century some German brewmasters came to the United States with the sole intention of setting up breweries. The Germans brought with them the new technique (at that time) of bottom fermentation, meaning that a yeast settles to the bottom of the brewing tank during fermentation. This process results in either *munchner, dortmunder,* or *pilsner* brews. Each brew is named after the town in Germany in which it was first brewed. Munchner is the darkest brew, and

Fig. 1-2. Most American beers taste the same, but the home brewer can make many different and good tasting beers.

pilsner is the lightest. Largely because of the pressures of standardization in America, the beers most commonly available are much lighter and less hopped than true pilsners (Fig. 1-2).

TOP AND BOTTOM FERMENTATION

Top fermentation is the major difference between European brewing and most American brewing processes. Top fermenting (a term used to describe the action of the yeast used in the process) means that the yeasts rise to the surface during the brewing process rather than lie on the bottom of the fermentation tank. Top-fermented beers come in many varieties from relatively pale ales to *porter* (a dark, heavy ale that is popular in Ireland) to *stout* (which is also very heavy and has a higher alcoholic content).

Top fermentation is the oldest type of brewing method. If the brewing beer could be kept cold during the process (about 5 degrees centigrade or 41 degrees Fahrenheit), it would not go sour. The finished beer would be much clearer. The spent yeast would gradually settle to the bottom of the cask. This discovery was made in and around the foothills of the Bavarian

Alps where casks of brewing beer were stored in caves and packed in natural ice.

With the development of artificial refrigeration in the 1800s, the bottom fermentation brewing process became universally used in the brewing industry. The action of yeast was being explained by Louis Pasteur around this time. The end result was the development of a yeast that naturally fermented on the bottom of the beer vat rather than on the top.

All beers produced in the United States generally are made with bottom-fermenting yeast, and all ales are made with top-fermenting yeast. There are a few exceptions to this rule—from small, local breweries. In Germany, Belgium, and northern France, top-fermented beer is brewed widely, but the brew itself is much more of an ale than a true beer.

COMMERCIAL BREWING STATISTICS

Americans currently consume approximately 22.5 gallons of beer annually, according to industry statistics. The United States ranks thirteenth in the world in beer consumption. West Germany has the highest consumption of beer, with an average of about 32 gallons per person (Fig. 1-3).

Brewing in the United States is big business—to the tune of about $16 million annually. The United States is the largest brewing nation (producing about 179.6 million hectoliters annually or about 157 million barrels). The three largest brewers—Anheuser-Busch, Schlitz, and Miller—produce roughly 50 percent of the beer consumed in the United States and export more than the total amount consumed.

The American brewing industry employs more than 50,000 people directly. Approximately 4 million acres of farmland are needed to grow malt (123 million bushels, with a value of $500 million). About $170 million worth of corn, wheat, and rice are used. The value of hops used in the annual production of beer (and other malt beverages) is around $30 million. The commercial brewers of the United States pay more than $1.4 billion annually in federal excise taxes and around $0.7 billion annually in state taxes.

More than $3 billion is spent annually by the brewing industry to purchase beer containers. Although the trend is changing,

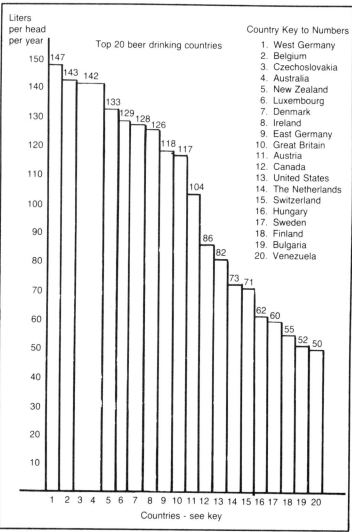

Fig. 1-3. Chart showing per capita consumption of beer.

more beer is sold in one-way containers (1.5 billion) than in returnable cans and bottles (570 million). Almost 90 percent of all beer produced in the United States is in cans or bottles (both one-way and returnable combined). The rest is offered for sale in kegs (largely to bars and restaurants). Approximately 25 percent of all commercial canning in the United States is for beer. In 1977 39 percent of all retail package sales were for beer—roughly 13 billion bottles and cans.

Roughly 90 percent of the commercially brewed beer in the United States is bottom-fermented. Because all bottom-fermented beers are considered lager, most of the beer produced in America can rightly be called lager.

There are several by-products in the brewing industry. Brewer's yeast is sold as a vitamin. It is rich in B-complex vitamins. Other by-products are the grains used in beer production—mainly barley, corn, rice, and other cereals. These by-products are sold by the breweries for livestock feed.

BREWING PROCESS

Brewing is really very simple on a small scale. It becomes more complex when you think in terms of millions of gallons of beer.

Mashing

The beer brewing process begins by mixing malt—barley that has been germinated—with hot water and allowing this mixture to stand for a short period. This process is called *mashing*, and it allows the malt enzymes to go to work and break down the polysaccharides. During the malting process grains such as corn or rice may be added to aid the breakdown of enzymes. These grain additives are commonly called *adjuncts*. The temperature of this mixture known as *wort* is controlled very carefully and maintained for a predetermined period.

After about one hour of mashing, the mixture is stabilized by heating it to a temperature of 175 degrees Fahrenheit. This halts the mashing process and destroys most of the enzymes in the wort.

The contents of the mashing tub then are transferred to the *lauter tub*. The lauter tub is a cylindrical tank with a false bottom of slotted plates through which the clear malt wort is run off. The cereal husks from adjuncts form a natural filter bed. After the wort has been filtered, the grain husks are washed with hot water. This liquid is added to the wort extract. At this time the cereal grains are no longer required for the brewing process and are commonly sold as livestock feed.

Adding Hops to the Wort

The wort is boiled for about one hour to destroy any remaining enzymes. Then hops are added to the boiling wort. The amount of hops and the time they are added depend on the beer being brewed. Many German beers (and American beers of similar strength) are hopped at the rate of about .5 pound of hops for each barrel of beer. English beers and ales commonly have more hops—up to about 1.5 pounds of hops per barrel, depending on type.

Hops are added to the wort primarily to give the characteristic aroma and taste of beer. Ales generally have a heavier hop taste and aroma. The amount of hops added frequently is a guarded secret of the brewmaster.

Hops are boiled in the wort for a period, and they give off a variety of substances. These include oils and complex bittering substances such as *humulone, cohumulone,* and *adhumulone*. These substances contribute to the flavor and aroma of the beer. The hops also give off *tannins*, which help to settle the beer and thus make it clear.

Adding Yeast to the Wort

The wort is then strained and cooled to around 40 degrees Fahrenheit. The yeast is added to the wort, and the liquid is placed in the *primary fermenter*. The first fermentation takes place and, depending on the type of yeast used, may be either beer or ale. Top-fermenting yeasts produce ale while bottom-fermenting yeasts produce beer. Most modern breweries now use a special yeast strain that is especially suited for brewing beer.

The yeast is allowed to work in the wort long enough to break down the sugars into alcohol. This period can be anywhere from six to nine days, and during this time the yeast organisms multiply about threefold. The wort's alcohol content at the end of this period is around 4 percent for lager beers and higher for ales. During this period the primary fermenter is kept at a constant temperature of 55 degrees Fahrenheit.

Lagering

The yeast will have settled to the bottom of the tank at the end of this primary fermentation. The liquid is now called *green beer*. It is siphoned off and pumped into another container—the *secondary fermenter*—where it is allowed to sit for several weeks. This settling is called *lagering*, and it permits the beer to mature. The yeast, which is left in the tank after siphoning, remains active and can be used repeatedly. Many modern breweries simply add a bit more yeast to this used yeast and use the mixture in the next batch of beer. Some yeast cultures are stronger than others and will last anywhere from several months to several years. Careful controls are required to prevent contamination of the yeast cultures between batches of beer.

After lagering, the beer is then filtered several times to remove all traces of particulate matter—yeast and fine protein. Then the beer is carbonated, most commonly with an

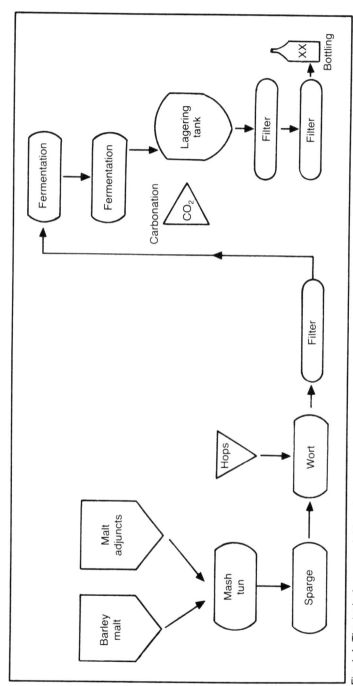

Fig. 1-4. The typical commercial brewing process.

10

injection of carbon dioxide, before bottling. Sometimes the beer undergoes another fermentation before bottling known as *krausening*.

Pasteurizing

The last step that most American beers undergo after bottling is pasteurizing. This is most commonly done by running the capped bottles and cans through a special tunnel where they are bathed in water at 140 degrees Fahrenheit for 15 to 20 minutes. Pasteurization is necessary to kill most of the microorganisms that can grow in beer and cause it to go sour. Beer in stainless steel or aluminum kegs is not pasteurized. It is kept refrigerated until used.

This description of modern commercial beer brewing is overly simplified, but the major steps have been included. When you begin to brew your own beer at home, you will follow this basic chain of procedures (Fig. 1-4).

ADDITIVES

The main difference between commercially brewed beer and ales and that which you will brew at home is marketing. American brewers must produce a beer that has pleasing characteristics such as a creamy white head, carbonation, pale golden color, long shelf life, and a beer that is as clear as fresh spring water. To create a beverage with these qualities and others, American brewers have turned to modern science and chemistry.

When you open a can of your favorite beer, you probably never think that there are chemicals and other additives inside. Many things are added to ensure that the brew inside lives up to your expectations. Presently more than 60 chemicals and additives can be added during the brewing and bottling process to impart various characteristics to the beer. When you first open the can, the beer does not gush out because a chemical, most commonly ethylenediaminetetraacetic acid, was added to prevent this outpouring. When you pour your beer into a glass, a great white head of foam sits on top of the liquid. Often this head is the result of a squirt of propylene glycol alginate or possibly gum arabic just before bottling.

Look at the beer itself. It will be very clear and (depending on brand) a shade of amber or gold in color. While these characteristics can be achieved through time at the brewery, many brewers speed up the process by adding *proteases*—enzymes that digest protein and thus clarify the beer—and food colorings such as caramel to give the beer a rich golden color.

When you sip commercial beer, you may be drinking more than the fermentation of water, hops, malt, and yeast. Any commercially made beer may contain potassium metabisulfite, octanal, adipic acid, ethyl maltol, malic acid, grapefruit oil, lemon oil, tartaric acid, ascorbic acid, and other additives. When you realize that none of these additives are required for brewing good beer, you will want to make your own beer if for no other reason than you will know what is in it.

AMERICAN BREWING INDUSTRY

The American brewing industry has an unusual position in the food and beverage industry. When almost all food products must adhere to strict labeling practices, this industry is not required to list ingredients used in beer making. On any given beer label you will see claims about artesian well water, Rocky Mountain spring water, the finest hops, old world brewing methods, etc., but you will not find any reference to chemicals or other additives. All commercial breweries use additives to achieve various qualities, but they are not required to list them (Fig. 1-5). If you would like more detailed information about beer additives, consult the *Congressional Record*, 12 March 1980, B 1471.

The political clout of the American brewing industry is tremendous in that they are not required to list ingredients on

Fig. 1-5. It is almost impossible to know what other ingredients are in your favorite commercial beer. American brewers are not required to list anything on their labels.

packaging. Unfortunately, this has led to several deaths in the past. At one time cobalt sulfate was used in commercial breweries because it produced a long lasting, foamy head on beer. Then it was discovered that cobalt sulfate caused heart attacks. More than 40 people died, and the only thing they had in common was beer drinking. The use of this chemical was banned in the industry.

In all fairness to the American brewing industry, I have written several letters asking for information about additives used in commercial brewing. I have also written to the American Brewers Association to get their input for this book. I have received no response to my queries, so I am led to believe that the brewers of the United States are unwilling to discuss the ways in which they make beer.

SUGAR

Sugar is used for several recipes in this book. Sugar is used in the home brewery to speed up fermentation and to increase the beer's alcohol content. Sugar is safe to use in brewing beer at home.

Equipment

Unless you are going into the brewing business for which you need a license, you only need a few specialized pieces of equipment for home brewing (Fig. 2-1). Probably you already own most of the containers, the boiling pot, thermometer, and other implements of brewing if you are reasonably active in the kitchen (Fig. 2-2). Other items are needed that are not found around the normal household such as a hydrometer, air locks, bottle capper, and siphon hose.

While you can make good beer for around 50¢ per quart, there are production expenses that will be more or less spread out over your beer making lifetime. The initial cost may set you back around $50. Once you have purchased a good bottle capper, costing anywhere from $7 to $40, you need never make the purchase again.

Shopping wisely is certainly one area where it is possible to cut costs. Shopping by mail is becoming popular. Substantial savings can be realized by buying caps, specialized brewer's yeast, and specific hops through a mail-order catalog. The Appendix lists addresses of firms with a mail-order line of products for the home brewer. Because some dealers pay

Fig. 2-1. The typical home brewery is not elaborate. With these simple tools, you can brew great tasting beer at a fraction of the cost of commercially brewed beer.

postage, it is usually possible to buy items such as 35-pound cans of malt extract syrup at a price lower than that of the beer and wine making supply shop in your area. Write for catalogs and compare those prices with what you are paying for basic materials (Fig. 2-3).

You may substitute equipment that will do the job but is not

Fig. 2-2. You may already have much of the brewing equipment needed around your home.

necessarily sold for the purpose of brewing. One good example is the primary fermenter. Any shop that sells beer and wine making supplies will have a line or two of fermentation tanks for beer. Plastic tanks cost from $5 to $20. Almost any 5-gallon container in clean, sound condition will do the job. I know several home brewers who use 20-gallon trash cans (purchased new for the purpose) as primary fermenters and

Fig. 2-3. Considerable savings on brewing materials and equipment can often be realized by shopping wisely through the mails.

5-gallon water bottles (purchased at the local flea market for $3 each) as secondary fermenters.

PRIMARY FERMENTER

The *primary fermenter* used for most home brewing is nothing more than a 5-gallon (or more) container. Many primary fermenters are available in beer and wine making supply stores with prices below $10. If you buy equipment at these stores, it will probably be "food grade" plastic and white in color. Many fermenters have lids that can be fastened securely (Fig. 2-4). Lids must be tight during brewing.

Before you use a primary fermenter or any other piece of equipment, it must be sterilized to kill any airborne yeast or bacteria. Failure to do this will most commonly result in beer that is dumped down the drain rather than being consumed. Another consideration is whether or not the primary fermenter can be sealed tightly to exclude the atmosphere, which contains airborne bacteria and yeasts that can ruin your beer. You can cover almost any container with a sheet of

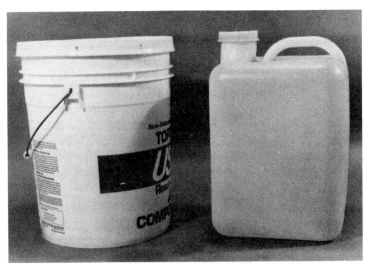

Fig. 2-4. A primary fermenter can be almost any 5-gallon (or more) container that can be sealed.

clean, clear plastic and secure the edges with tape. Some type of screw-down lid is preferable.

I have seen several containers used as primary fermenters with varying rates of success. Some better containers for brewing include new plastic trash cans, baby diaper pails (with lids) 5-gallon plastic water bottles, and recycled aluminum (or stainless steel) beer kegs.

SECONDARY FERMENTER

The most popular *secondary fermenter* is a 5-gallon water bottle often called a glass *carboy*. These containers can be cleaned with a long-handled bottle brush and are readily available. Almost any beer and wine making supply shop will sell them for around $10 to $15. You can usually find them for much lower prices at garage sales or your local flea market. A fermentation air lock, fitted into a single hole rubber stopper (number 6.5 or 7), will fit almost any of these bottles. It is very easy to seal the brew from the atmosphere (Fig. 2-5).

Alternatives to the glass carboy include plastic jugs designed for brewing or any other container that can be sealed with an airlock (Fig. 2-6). If you use plastic containers for either the primary or secondary fermenter, you should neutralize the inside by washing with bicarbonate of soda and water. Rinse thoroughly before using.

BOILING POT

A *boiling pot* is used for boiling the wort prior to siphoning into the primary fermenter. Almost any large pot will do if it holds at least 2 gallons of liquid comfortably. A larger capacity pot is preferable, though.

A standard canning pot is ideal if the enamel is not chipped or cracked inside. A stainless steel pot with a large capacity is even better. A pot in which the wort is boiled must be

Fig. 2-5. A secondary fermenter must be fitted with a special air lock to seal out the atmosphere.

completely free of grease or any other residue before use. Scrub the pot, then sterilize it with sodium metabisulfite just prior to use (Fig. 2-7).

FERMENTATION LOCK

A *fermentation lock* or *air lock* is placed on top of the secondary fermenter during fermentation. Almost all fermentation locks are partially filled with water, which acts as a one-way seal on the container. This seal permits the escape of carbon dioxide that is generated during fermentation and prevents the atmosphere from entering. There are many styles of air locks on the market, and all work about the same (Fig. 2-8). Plastic air locks are probably the best, but the fancy imported glass air locks are attractive (and overpriced, as a rule).

Fig. 2-6. Even a 5-gallon plastic jug can be used as a secondary fermenter if it can be fitted with an air lock.

Fig. 2-7. A large canning pot is handy for boiling the wort.

SIPHON HOSE AND SIPHONING

Siphon hose is used for transferring liquids from one container to another—from primary fermenter to secondary fermenter, for example—and for bottling your beer after fermentation has stopped. The reason for siphoning rather than pouring is to reduce contact with the atmosphere during these operations. Also, you can transfer liquids and simultaneously leave settling in the bottom of the container. This is done by lowering the siphon hose gradually, as the liquid level drops, until you have siphoned off almost all the liquid but not the sediment at the bottom of the container (Fig. 2-9).

Clear plastic ⅜-inch hose is the best siphon hose. This is available at any beer and wine making supply store and many other places. The current price is around 20¢ per foot. A 6-foot length is ideal for the home brewer (Fig. 2-10).

A special clamp is used for starting and stopping the flow of beer in the hose. These clamps are available at beer and wine making supply stores and currently cost about 50¢. You will

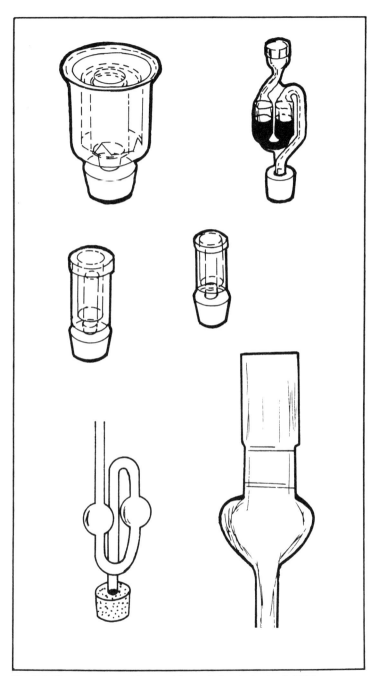

Fig. 2-8. There are several types of fermentation locks or air locks.

Fig. 2-9. Siphoning is the easiest way of transferring liquids.

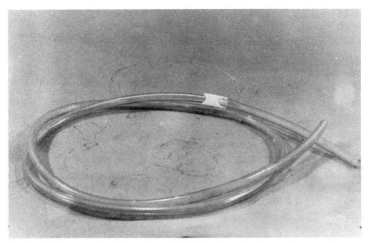

Fig. 2-10. Clear plastic siphon hose (⅜ inch in diameter) is easily available and will do a good job of siphoning.

appreciate this aid on your first bottle filling operation (Fig. 2-11).

Your goal when siphoning is to transfer as much of the clear liquor as possible with little particulate matter—such as yeast cultures and hop fragments. You probably will not perfect this technique until you have siphoned a few batches of beer.

Begin by inserting one end of your hose through the fermenter's neck. Hold one finger over the opposite end, which will help to create a partial vacuum in the hose. Lower the end of the hose down about 4 inches into the liquor and rotate it, if necessary, so that the end appears along the container's side. This enables you to see the depth of the hose at all times and makes it easy for you to drop the tip down lower as the container drains (Fig. 2-12).

Remove your finger from the free end of the hose and bring the end to your mouth. A slight sucking action will start the liquor up and through the hose. Ideally, the container you are emptying should be higher than the new container. As the

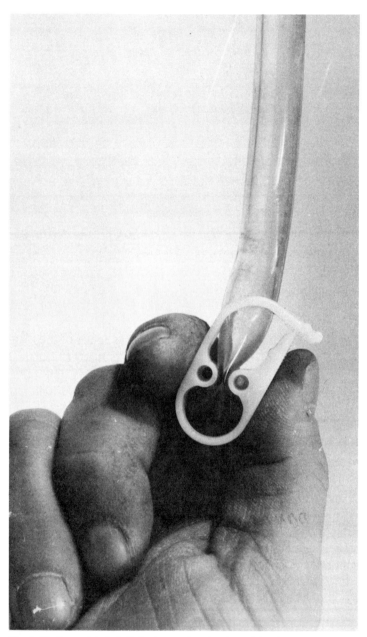

Fig. 2-11. A special shutoff clip is very handy when siphoning.

Fig. 2-12. Turn the inflow end of the siphon hose toward the side of the container so you can see what is flowing into the hose.

27

liquor starts to run down the tube, place the end into the new container. The siphoning action should be in progress.

There are two things to be conscious of when siphoning beer. The first is to closely watch the flow of liquor into the tube. You are siphoning beer and not sediment. The end of the hose must not draw from the bottom area of the fermentation tank, either primary or secondary fermenter, until the level of the liquor is low. Lower the end of the hose very carefully until you begin to see sediment flowing, then stop your siphoning. It is false economy to siphon yeast or other sediment as these particles do nothing good for the appearance or taste of your beer.

The second thing involves the outflowing liquor. Whenever you open up a fermentation vessel to siphon, the liquor comes in contact with airborne yeasts and bacteria that will infect your beer. Do not allow the outflowing beer to splash; hold the tip of the hose at the top of the new container. Instead, lower the outflow end to the bottom of the new container. This goes for siphoning from one fermenter to another or from the secondary fermenter into bottles.

BOTTLES

The biggest headache you will encounter in home brewing is finding enough *bottles*. For starters, you will need enough bottles for about 5 gallons of beer. About 20-quart bottles (1.75 cases) or about 54 12-ounce bottles (just over two cases) are needed. Beer should sit for at least five weeks before opening, so you will probably want to have enough bottles for several batches. One brewing friend claims to have almost 1,000 bottles around the house that are used primarily for beer, although some bottles are also used for root beer, apple cider, and other beverages.

Finding bottles for beer can be challenging as you never seem to have enough. It used to be possible to find beer in quart

Fig. 2-13. Finding suitable bottles for home brewing is a challenge.

bottles with crown caps. These bottles are still available in some parts of the country, but they generally carry a deposit of 5¢ to 25¢. Any large bottle of almost any capacity that can be capped with a crown cap is suitable for bottling home brew. Many returnable soda pop bottles are suitable. If you are starting a collection, green or dark brown glass bottles are more desirable than clear glass ones (Figs. 2-13 and 2-14).

Your beer bottle collection should consist of bottles of various sizes. Quart bottles are probably best, but 12-ounce bottles are more readily available.

Moving both empty and full beer bottles around is a chore. Store all bottles in cases or carrying cartons. It is far easier to move one case of beer rather than 12 quarts or 24 bottles. Because cases for empty bottles can be difficult to obtain, you should have six-packs for bottles—either quart or 12-ounce sizes. These cardboard carriers are commonly available in supermarkets, but you may have to ask for them (Fig. 2-15).

In addition to buying beverages in reusable bottles, you can also try local taverns and restaurants. Because many imported beers such as Lowenbrau and Heinekin come in crown-capped bottles that are commonly thrown away, you can reuse these containers if you can obtain them. Try asking someone in a position of authority if you can have these empties or purchase them for a very small fee. A brewing friend was offered more than 20 cases of empty bottles for the price of hauling them away. Check empty bottles very carefully and wash them with chemical cleaners.

Fig. 2-14. Screwtop bottles are not suitable for recapping.

Fig. 2-15. Special carrying cases for bottles enable you to handle several bottles at once.

BOTTLE BRUSHES

When cleaning fermenters and bottles, a long-handled *bottle brush* is indispensable for scrubbing out foreign matter. Always rinse out beer bottles after decanting the beer. Sometimes you will forget, or rinsing out a bottle may just not be possible. Then you will have to scrub the residue inside the bottles with a good brush before you refill the container (Fig. 2-16).

There are a few bottle washing gizmos currently available (Fig. 2-17). Some hook up to the kitchen faucet and force a stream of water inside the container being cleaned. A simple valve opens the flow of water when it is pressed against the inside bottom of the bottle, and it stops the flow when removed. These gadgets are handy providing there is not any

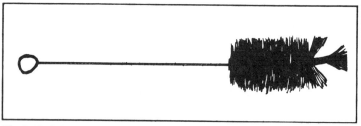

Fig. 2-16. A long-handled bottle brush is used to easily clean bottles.

dried residue in the bottom or along the sides of the bottle. If there is, a good bottle brush is about the only cleaning aid that really works.

Long-handled bottle brushes are commonly available at any store selling beer and wine making supplies and through mail-order companies (Fig. 2-18). Try bending the wire to make cleaning the shoulders of the glass carboy easier. When finished, simply bend the wire back to the original straight shape (Fig. 2-19).

For smaller bottles (quarts and less capacity), a smaller brush is much easier to use. Several types are available in beer and wine making supply shops, but you can usually do a good job with a baby bottle brush, which is available for a substantially lower cost (Fig. 2-20). The brush must be long enough to reach the bottom of any bottle. The tip of the brush must be narrow enough to fit down the neck of the bottle being scrubbed.

Fig. 2-17. Special bottle washers are available from beer and wine making supply stores.

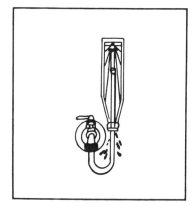

Fig. 2-18. A selection of bottle brushes will help you clean almost any container.

Fig. 2-19. You can easily bend the shaft of a bottle brush to help in cleaning all interior surfaces of any size bottle.

2-20. Use a small baby bottle brush for cleaning small bottles.

STERILIZING AGENTS

Your main aim when cleaning fermenters or bottles is to provide a sterile container for the incoming brew. In most cases it is unwise to rely solely on water for this cleaning. A stronger cleaner should be used—one that will not affect the beer in any manner. Common dishwashing soap will not sterilize containers. When some soaps are used on plastic containers, the plastic will retain the flavor of the soap being used. This is true of the lemon-scented dish soaps on the market.

A much better way to clean and sterilize fermenters and bottles used in brewing is to use one or more of the special sterilizing agents designed for the purpose. Sodium metabisulfite, sodium bisulfite, and campden tablets (which are made from sodium bisulfite) are the most popular types of chemical sterilizing compounds. These are available through beer and wine making supply stores and through mail order. You should have these chemicals around the home brewery. Use them carefully whenever a new container is pressed into service.

To use these sterilizing chemicals, you must first make up a dilute solution. In most cases begin by dissolving 2 teaspoons of the chemical in 2 quarts of warm water. You can increase the output of sulfur dioxide by adding a pinch of citric acid to this sterilizing solution. The release of sulfur dioxide does the sterilizing. Bathe the equipment in this sterilizing solution for 5 to 10 minutes, then rinse thoroughly in hot water to remove the sterilizing solution. Use the containers or bottles while they are still warm (Fig. 2-21).

This sterilizing technique should be followed prior to transferring beer from one fermenter to another or before bottling. This will do much to improve the overall success of your brewing. There will be times when this sterilizing method will not adequately do the job—heavily soiled bottles, for example. You must then resort to stronger sterilizing techniques—specifically, the use of chlorine bleach.

One of the most powerful sterilizing solutions can be made by diluting 2 tablespoons of household bleach in 2 quarts of water. Use this solution to soak badly soiled bottles and fermenters. Scrub if necessary to remove all grime. Rinse the container with hot water until all traces of the bleach have been removed. The main problem with this extremely powerful sterilizing solution is that it is difficult to rinse off totally, and your beer may suffer. Make up a solution of sodium metabisulfite or sodium bisulfite and rinse the container (or bottles) in this solution. These sodium-based sterilizing solutions will neutralize completely the chlorine bleach (Fig. 2-22).

For bottles that have been rinsed after opening and do not contain any dried residue inside, use your dishwasher to clean and sterilize the bottles just prior to filling. You can save yourself plenty of work. Inspect the interiors of all bottles for any residue. If you find any, remove it with a bottle brush and warm water. Place the bottles in the bottom tray of your dishwasher with the tops pointing down. Run the dishwasher through the rinse and dry cycle. The bottles will come out clean, dry, and ready for use.

Fig. 2-21. Bottles must be rinsed thoroughly after soaking in a sterilizing solution.

Fig. 2-22. Mix 2 tablespoons of household bleach in .5 gallon of water for a very strong sterilizing solution.

Use containers and bottles as soon as possible after sterilizing. The longer you wait to use the containers after sterilizing, the greater the chances are that they will become contaminated again. The beer being transferred into these new containers may become contaminated and be of poor quality.

BLENDER

If you will be making beer and ale from whole grains, you will need some special equipment. Because the grain kernels must be ground into fine particles, you need some type of crusher or grinder. One method of grinding whole grains that works well is to place small amounts of the grain in a *blender*. Turn the machine on and off quickly until the grain has been ground to a consistency like cornmeal (Fig. 2-23).

Fig. 2-23. Grain can be pulverized in a blender.

Fig. 2-24. After mashing, the grain is rinsed several times in a colander.

MASH TUN

After the grain has been ground properly, it must then be cooked in a large pot with hot water (from 110 to 150 degrees Fahrenheit). This pot is called a *mash tun*. Any 8-quart or larger cooking pot will suffice. If an enameled canning pot is used, be sure there are no chips or cracks in the interior.

COLANDER

After the grain is mashed, it must then be rinsed thoroughly to obtain all the malt extract that seems to adhere to the grain. This large-scale operation is known as *sparging* in the brewing industry. The best way for you to accomplish sparging is to simply run all the mash through a wire strainer or *colander*. Rinse the grain several times by pouring boiling water through the strainer. This liquor is added to the wort, which is then boiled with hops to obtain a brewing liquor (Fig. 2-24).

THERMOMETER

When malting whole grains, you need a *thermometer* for

measuring the temperature of the liquid during the process. Certain enzymes break down within specific temperature ranges. Protein modification takes place around 110 degrees Fahrenheit, while starch conversion takes place between 130 and 155 degrees Fahrenheit. Any thermometer with a range up to about 200 degrees Fahrenheit should do, but thermometers that float are best (Fig. 2-25).

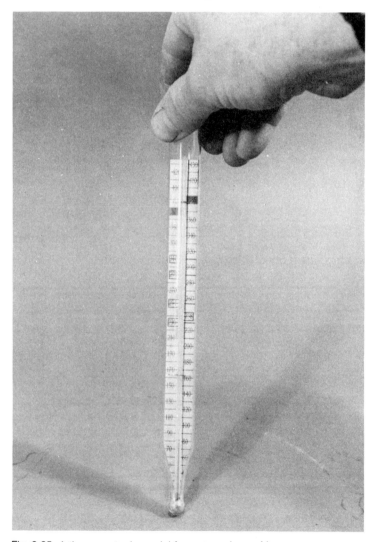

Fig. 2-25. A thermometer is crucial for success in mashing.

Fig. 2-26. Cheesecloth is a useful material for filtering when placed in a funnel.

CHEESECLOTH

Another filtering aid that is useful for many tasks around the home brewery is common *cheesecloth*. When straining the wort from the boiling pot into the primary fermenter, there will be a large quantity of hop and grain residue. If the hops are left in the wort, the liquor tends to be bitter. While this is permissible for stout, it is not desirable for pale lager beers. Because much of this material is in suspension in the wort, you must strain carefully. While you can use a metal strainer for the larger pieces of hop fragments, most of this material will pass through the mesh in the strainer. The best way to filter this material is through cheesecloth. Use fresh pieces of cheesecloth after about every gallon of wort has been filtered. The cheesecloth has a tendency to clog easily with the tiny particles of hop fragments. Hold the cheesecloth either over a large funnel or in a metal strainer or colander (Fig. 2-26).

HYDROMETER

About the only specialized piece of testing equipment you need is a *hydrometer*. A hydrometer is a simple instrument that measures the density of a liquid as compared with the density of pure water. This measurement is expressed as the specific gravity of the liquid being tested; pure water has a specific gravity of 1.000. When a hydrometer is floated in a container of water (a special testing jar or test tube is used), the level of the water will be at about 1.000. When the same instrument is floated in liquor from the secondary fermenter, the reading should be around 1.004. Testing wort—as it goes into the primary fermenter—should result in a reading of approximately 1.040 (Fig. 2-27).

When using a hydrometer, remember that a sugar solution such as wort is heavier than water. The hydrometer will float higher in it. As the sugar solution is converted to alcohol, the hydrometer will sink lower and lower until a reading of approximately 1.004 is achieved. Then it is time to bottle the brew.

Almost all hydrometers are designed to give accurate measurements of specific gravity when the temperature of the liquid is at 60 degrees Fahrenheit. If the temperature of the liquid is 10 or more degrees away from 60 degrees Fahrenheit, you must make adjustments to the reading. Figure 2-28 will aid you in making corrections to the hydrometer reading at various temperatures.

If you purchase a hydrometer new, you will undoubtedly receive instructions. In addition to these basic directions, there are two possible causes of errors for which you should be on the lookout. The first cause of error readings results from air bubbles that often adhere to the sides of the hydrometer. These air bubbles will cause the hydrometer to float higher in the container or test tube. The reading will be higher than it should be. To prevent this problem from occurring, you can simply give the hydrometer a spin with your thumb and index finger. This action will spin off the air bubbles and allow the hydrometer to float naturally, resulting in a true reading (Fig. 2-29).

Another common cause of erroneous hydrometer readings is directly related to the *meniscus effect*. If you look carefully at the hydrometer as it floats in the liquid inside the test container, notice that the liquid tends to creep up slightly along the sides of the hydrometer. Take a reading across the level of

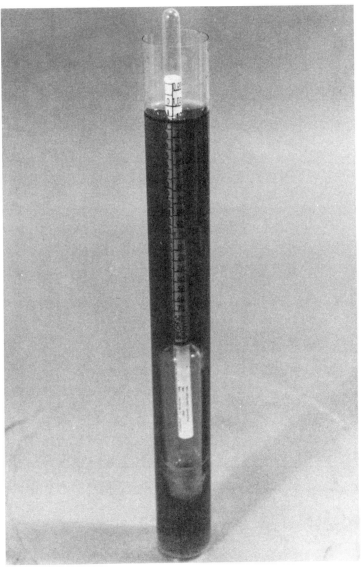

Fig. 2-27. A hydrometer is used in the brewing process.

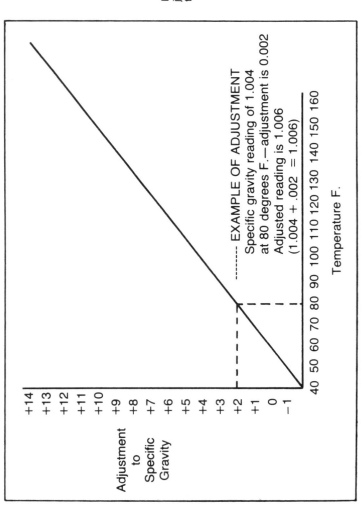

Fig. 2-28. Hydrometer reading adjustments for temperature variations.

EXAMPLE OF ADJUSTMENT
Specific gravity reading of 1.004
at 80 degrees F.—adjustment is 0.002
Adjusted reading is 1.006
(1.004 + .002 = 1.006)

Adjustment to Specific Gravity

+14
+13
+12
+11
+10
+9
+8
+7
+6
+5
+4
+3
+2
+1
0
−1

40 50 60 70 80 90 100 110 120 130 140 150 160

Temperature F.

Fig. 2-29. Spin the hydrometer to dislodge air bubbles around it.

the liquid, not at the height of where the liquid crept up. A higher reading will be obtained if you do not follow this advice.

BOTTLE CAPPER

Several bottle capping machines are available with prices

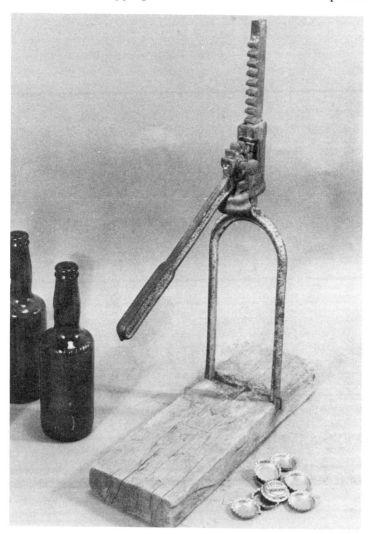

Fig. 2-30. A bottle capper machine.

Fig. 2-31. Crown caps.

ranging from around $10 for a hand-operated model to more than $30 for the super deluxe bench-mounted model. I feel that the least expensive bottle cappers are the best, simply because they cap quite well and are designed to last a long time (Fig. 2-30).

You may find a used model at a flea market or garage sale. One brewing friend has some new and antique bottle cappers that have been purchased at secondhand sales. The most expensive unit cost about $5.

CROWN CAPS

Crown caps for bottling beer are readily available from beer and wine making supply shops and mail-order companies. These caps are selling for about $1.50 per pound. Sometimes it is possible to pick up crown caps for a lower price. The newer crown caps are lined with plastic; older versions are lined with cork. Inspect caps before buying. Discard any caps that have scratches inside (Fig. 2-31).

LOGBOOK

You should keep some type of diary or log of ingredients used (such as brand and amount of hops) and other important information. Accurate records will enable you to decide on what ingredients are best according to your tastes.

While a beer log can be as simple and brief as you want, it will be more useful if you include as much information as possible. Certain facts must always be listed so you will have a sound basis for comparison. List all ingredients used and the amounts. Figure 2-32 is a sample of the kind of information that you should record.

Notice in Fig. 2-32 that starting and bottling dates are included. This will give you an indication of just how long it takes to brew good beer. Try varying the amount of time the beer is left in both the primary and secondary fermenter just to see if this makes an appreciable difference in the final brew. I record the specific gravity reading of the wort and also for the liquor just prior to bottling.

There are also columns for ingredients—hops, malt, and yeast—that are used for all batches of beer. Record the specific types used for any given batch of beer. I have found that some hops are better than others, so I use only those that produce the most pleasing taste. When a new brand of hops comes onto the market, I note this in my logbook and use this information as a basis for comparison.

Here's some other information that you may want to record: price paid for ingredients, temperature of brew at bottling time and of the room where beer is fermented, whether or not you have used finishing hops during the last few minutes of boiling the wort, and any other information that will enable you to brew better beer.

LIST
This list includes the equipment for brewing beer at home.
☐ Large pot for boiling wort.
☐ Primary fermenter—5-gallon size with lid.

Date	Malt Extract (Brand)	Hops (Brand & Type)	Whole Grains (Type & Weight)	Yeast (Brand)	Other Ingredients	S Gravity				Date Bottled	Remarks
						Wort	Prim	Secnd	Bottling		

Fig. 2-32. A sample page for a brewer's logbook.

- [ ] Secondary fermenter—5-gallon.
- [ ] Fermentation lock with rubber stopper.
- [ ] Siphon hose.
- [ ] Siphon hose clamp.
- [ ] Thermometer.
- [ ] Hydrometer.
- [ ] Bottle brushes.
- [ ] Cleaning chemicals.
- [ ] Empty bottles for 5 gallons of beer.
- [ ] Bottle capping machine or device.
- [ ] Bottle caps.
- [ ] Long-handled wooden spoon for stirring the boiling wort.
- [ ] Strainer and cheesecloth.
- [ ] Funnel.
- [ ] Measuring cup.
- [ ] Measuring spoons.
- [ ] Logbook.

Ingredients

As mentioned earlier, the basic ingredients for brewing beer are water, malt, malt adjuncts, hops, and yeast. While high-quality beers are brewed with these five ingredients all over the world, other ingredients can be added to either speed up the brewing process (sugar) or impart unique flavors to a particular batch of beer (spruce essence).

WATER

Water makes up the largest part of any beer or ale (about 90 percent). The quality of the water used in the brewing process will have a direct effect on the overall quality of the beer being brewed (Fig. 3-1).

The claims that modern commercial breweries make about the water they use should give you a clue as to the importance of this ingredient. Some brewers claim that their beer is made from "pure Rocky Mountain spring water." Others simply say, "from the land of sky blue water" or, "It's in the water." Commercial brewers do not refer to water when describing their particular brewing process. Instead they refer to it as liquor. Some brewers claim that water is used for washing out

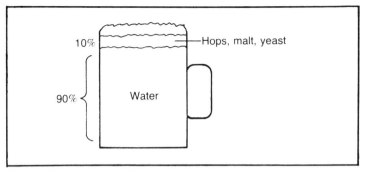

10% ──Hops, malt, yeast

90% { Water

Fig. 3-1. Water makes up 90 percent of any beer.

brewing tanks and equipment. Actually there is no such thing as the all-purpose water for brewing beer and ale.

The founders of breweries around the world quickly realized that some water supplies were more suitable than others for brewing certain beers and ales. This rule holds true today. Water that is hard or high in mineral elements has a pH value above 7.0. This type of water is better suited for brewing dark beers and ales. Soft water containing a few mineral elements has a pH value below 7.0 and is suitable for brewing light beers. Soft water (ph 1.0-7.0) is acid. Hard water (pH 7.0-4.0) is alkaline. Water with a pH value of 7.0 is neutral.

The pH of the water used in brewing can affect the taste of the finished product. Commercial brewers and beverage bottlers filter, sterilize, or otherwise treat all water used in the brewing of beer. Constant testing and adjustments are common in the industry. The pH of the liquor is ideal for the particular process underway. During mashing, for example, the overall pH should be around 5.2. When more liquor is added to the batch, the pH should be neutral or 7.0.

You need not necessarily concern yourself with the pH of the water being used for brewing beer. Most municipal water supplies are on the soft side, with a pH of around 6.0 or slightly acid. Water around this pH value is almost perfect for brewing beer and ale. There is little need for attempting to change or modify the overall pH by adding salts or gypsum. If the water in your area is not soft, you may want to take some actions to achieve a good overall pH in the water used for brewing your own beer.

One simple test that will give you a general idea as to the softness or hardness of your water supply involves using common hand soap. Wet your hands and lather up with a bar of soap. If you can easily produce plenty of suds and lather, then your water is on the soft or acid side and has a pH less than 7.0. If your washing produces very little or no lather, then your water is alkaline or hard and has a pH greater than 7.0.

If you can produce a lather with ordinary hand soap and tap water, the water is suitable for brewing beer at home. If you find lather hard to achieve, then your beer will probably benefit from the addition of a water conditioner designed specifically to increase the acidity and to soften the water.

There are several ways you can deal with a problem water supply for brewing; problem water supply in this case means water that is either too hard or too soft. The first and simplest approach is to do nothing. Brew up a batch of beer. Wait several weeks for the beer to age properly, then taste it. If the beer tastes good and you are reasonably content with it, continue brewing beer without any more thought to the water you are using. If you find that the taste of the beer is too light or a little sour, you may want to treat the water that will be used in the next batch of beer to see if this makes any difference in the beer's overall quality. Other factors can affect the taste of your beer such as unsterile fermenting tanks and bottles, poor-quality hops, and cooking the hops too long in the wort mixture.

Before you can change the pH of the water that will be used for brewing, you must first find out what the pH of the existing water is. The simplest way to accomplish this is to have your water tested by a reliable source. In most cities and towns a water testing service is performed by the local water works. If you have city water in your home, it will be a simple matter of finding out how to have your household water tested. You usually will be billed annually for this service. Look at the most current bill to learn where the water works is located. Call them and ask to have your water tested. A fellow from the local water works came to my home and tested the water right in my kitchen. Sometimes you may have to bring a water sample down to the water works. The local water company can tell you exactly what the pH of your domestic water supply is. If you ask, you should quickly learn what you must add to 5 gallons of water to develop an ideal pH for brewing beer.

If you live out in the country, you may have a bit of difficulty in learning the pH of your water supply. The hardness or softness of your water—if it comes from an underground well—is determined by the minerals in the soil in your area. Have a water sample tested by a reliable source. Check your Yellow Pages under the headings of Agricultural Extension Office, Department of Agriculture, and possibly local colleges or universities. Finding a testing source is the most difficult part. When you locate someone to do the testing, you can take appropriate action to develop the ideal pH for the water used in your home brewing. Water testing kits—strips of paper that are dipped in water and change color, according to the hardness or softness of the water you are testing—are of value to you. These water pH test kits are commonly available from beer and wine making supply shops and through mail order.

If you are using canned malt extract, the pH of brewing water will not matter much unless it is very hard or very soft. When you are making your own malt by mashing grain, the overall pH of your brewing water becomes much more crucial to success.

Mashing—the process of cooking malted barley in water to convert the grain starches to fermentable sugars and nonfermentable dextrins—requires water that is slightly acid, with a pH of about 5.0. Because most domestic water supplies in the United States are around pH 7.0 or near neutral, you must adjust the overall pH of water used in mashing, or there will not be enough acid for the conversion. Assuming that your water supply is around pH 7.0, you must add water hardeners such as Burton water salts or gypsum to the water used in the mashing process. You can also add citric acid to the water—1 to 2 teaspoons per 5 gallons of water—to increase the overall acid (lower the pH) of the water. More details will be given later in this chapter on adjusting the pH of the water used in this advanced brewing process.

MALT

All beers and ales use malt during the early stages of the brewing process. Barley is a grain that has been used for brewing beer for around 6,000 years. Some historians suggest that barley was grown in ancient civilizations solely for the purpose of brewing beer. Friezes depicting the entire brewing process have been found in Egyptian tombs. The word beer comes from the Saxon word for barley: *baere*.

Barley

Presently three types of barley are grown in the world, but only about one-tenth of the barley produced is used for brewing. Barley types are distinguished according to the number of rows of grain on each ear. Two-rowed barley is the most widely grown in Europe. Six-rowed barley can be grown in warm climates, and this type is good for malting. This barley is grown in the western United States, Chile, Australia, and the Mediterranean region. Four-rowed barley can be grown only in cold northern climates. Because of its high protein content, four-row barley is less suitable for brewing than the other types. It is not commonly used in the brewing process (Fig. 3-2).

Barley is an ideal grain for brewing, but it must be malted before the food reserves in each grain can be used. This is accomplished by germinating the grain. When germination begins, the shoot of the developing plant travels inside the grain where it is protected for several days until it finally emerges at the far end of the grain. When other grains germinate such as rye, wheat, and corn, the new shoot sprouts directly out and can be broken off easily before the internal food supply can be converted. Barley is the most suitable of all grains for brewing.

The very first step in the brewing process is to germinate the barley. This malting process is done by first crushing the grain, then mixing with hot water and letting the mixture sit for 30 minutes to one hour. In commercial brewing, this is commonly referred to as a "resting" period. If malt adjuncts such as corn or other cereal grains are to be added, these are also germinated in another container and added to the mash after about 30 minutes. The addition of adjuncts imparts no flavor to the overall mash, but it helps to increase the volume of fermentable sugars in the mash.

Fig. 3-2. Amber malted barley grains.

The mixture is kept at 157 degrees Fahrenheit for one hour. It is then heated to 175 degrees Fahrenheit. This temperature will destroy most of the enzymes that have formed in the mash. This process is technically known as *mashing off*.

After mashing off, the mixture is transferred to the *lauter tub*. Lauter means clear in German. A commercial lauter tub is a cylindrical tank with a false bottom of slotted plates through which the malt liquid is run off. The husks of the grain in the bottom of the lauter tub form a natural and very effective filtering device for the liquid or wort. After the mash has been strained and filtered, the husks are washed or sparged with hot water to add to the wort's volume. The spent grains are commonly sold as livestock feed.

Canned Malt Extracts

You have two basic choices concerning the malt you will use. The first and simplest is canned malt extract. Many excellent malt extracts are available. Part of the appeal of canned malt extract is that the steps previously mentioned for malting barley grain have been done for you by the experts. To make beer, you simply begin by boiling water and adding canned malt extract. There is no need to concern yourself with the pH of your water, quality of the barley grain, specific temperatures, sparging, or cattle feed. I highly recommend canned malt extract for the beginning brewer. You can experiment later with malting your own grain. Many experts feel that this gives you much more control over the finished product, so you will probably want to try malting as you polish up your brewing skills.

Many commercial breweries around the world also rely on malt extract rather than malting barley themselves. Some large malt extract syrup makers—German, Dutch, Canadian, and American—supply extract to commercial (both large and small) breweries and also offer small quantities for retail sale. These types can be found in your local or mail-order beer and wine supply houses.

A local shop in my area offers more then 30 types of malt extract syrup. You may be easily confused when making your first few purchases of malt extract syrup. You really have no way of knowing what you are getting or what you really like until you have tried a few. I strongly recommend that you stick with the suggestions given in this book's basic beer brewing recipes.

Blue Ribbon malt extract syrups are probably the most popular. They are also the least expensive. The current price for a 3-pound can is around $4.50. Most imported malt extract syrups retail for around $8 per 3.5-pound can. At one time Blue Ribbon malt extract syrups were available in most supermarkets, but now this is generally not the case except in rural areas. Part of the reason is the trend toward buying commercial beer rather than making beer at home. These malt extract syrups are available in unhopped and hopped light and dark malt syrup.

Another American malt extract syrup line is made by Super-brau. This company offers a wide line of extracts, yeast, hops, and other ingredients and supplies for beer makers. Super-brau malt extracts are commonly premixed with corn syrup. This eliminates the need for adding corn sugar to the beer recipe. They are sold in 5.1-pound cans. Each can of Super-brau malt extract syrup is sufficient for making 5 gallons of beer. Hopped, unhopped, light, amber, and dark malt extract syrups are available.

Many fine malt extract syrups are imported from England. John Bull and Munton & Fison are probably the most popular. John Bull malt extract syrups are sold in 3.3-pound cans (Fig. 3-3). Munton & Fison syrups are sold in 3.5-pound cans. Both brands are sufficient for making 5-gallon batches of beer. They are available in hopped, unhopped, light, amber, and dark varieties. Imported malt extract syrups are around twice the price of American-made malt extract syrups. The imported brands of malt extract syrups produce a different tasting brew than the American versions. Some home brew-

Fig. 3-3. Canned malt extract syrup.

ers like the taste of imported malt brewed beer better than beer made with domestic malt. Do your own taste testing to discover which brands and types you favor.

Bulk Malt Extract

Another malt extract syrup is sold in bulk from 50-gallon drums. Only large beer and wine making supply stores will have this malt extract syrup, and they will usually sell it by the pound. The current retail price is around $1.25 a pound. If available, you should purchase 3 or 3.5 pounds and make a test batch of beer. If you are satisfied with the quality of the brew, buy the malt extract syrup in larger quantities.

WHOLE GRAINS

While totally acceptable beers can be brewed with malt extract syrups, eventually you will probably want to try mashing your own barley. This is an area where even the experienced brewer can become confused.

Pale Malt

The most popular barley grain for home and commercial

brewing is called *pale malt* (or pale malted barley). Pale malt is simply barley grain that has been malted (Fig. 3-4). Malting is not a process that is carried out by the home brewer (or in many cases the commercial brewer). It is left to the experts.

The malting process begins by steeping raw barley grains in warm water until they germinate or sprout. During this germination process two important enzymes are produced—*amylase* and *proteinase*. The amylase enzymes can convert starches into other substances (at specific temperatures) when activated. The proteinase enzymes can break down proteins at certain temperatures. The amylase enzymes are made up of two components—alpha-amylase and beta-amylase. Alpha-amylase is most active at around 150-155 degrees Fahrenheit. It can convert starch to maltose sugar and nonfermentable dextrins. Beta-amylase converts starch to fermentable maltose sugar when the temperature is from 130 to 140 degrees Fahrenheit. The proteinase enzyme is active at temperatures of 115 to 120 degrees Fahrenheit.

The basic malting process must be carried out for all barley grains used in brewing. By varying the length of the process, it is possible to achieve two types of malted grain. As the germination process proceeds, the proteinase enzyme converts more and more of the protein, but the overall strength of the amylase enzyme decreases. If germination is halted early before all protein materials are converted, the resulting malt will be high in amylase strength. It will also have a large

Fig. 3-4. Pale, amber, and black malted barley grains.

amount of unconverted protein. When the germination process is halted early, the malt is called *undermodified*. This is the most common malting process in the United States.

The germination process is commonly allowed to proceed further in Europe and England. The end result is a malt that is low in amylase strength but has most of the protein converted. This type of malt is called *fully modified*.

Commercial breweries in the United States use malt adjuncts (corn and rice, for example) with undermodified malted barley grains. These adjuncts are converted to sugar by the high amylase strength of the malt. The home brewer must know which type of malted barley is being used.

Pale malt is composed of approximately 70 percent starch (by weight) and is the basic ingredient for making all grain beers. The designation grain beers is used for brews that are made from malted barley (most commonly pale malt) rather than brews made from malt extract syrup.

Crystal Malt

Crystal malt and *black malt* are colored malts that are generally available to the home and commercial brewer.

Crystal malt differs from pale malt in that it is amber in color and slightly sweeter. Crystal malt is processed so that most of the starch in the grain has been converted to sugar. The grain is roasted lightly to give a distinct amber color. Crystal malt is used in small amounts, almost always in conjunction with pale malt, to add color and flavor to beer and ale. It is not usually mashed in the same manner as pale malt. It is added to the boiling wort.

Black Malt

Black malt is simply barley grain that has been heavily roasted to achieve a black or dark brown color. Black malt is

Fig. 3-5. Corn is a malt adjunct.

used as coloring and flavoring additive in brews made basically with pale malt. It is used only in the darkest beers and stouts and has a very strong flavor.

Corn

Other grains that may be used in brewing beer are commonly called malt adjuncts. Corn and rice are the most popular (Fig. 3-5). Adjuncts are used as a source of starch, which is converted to sugar by the enzymes in the malted barley. They do not add any other characteristic to the beer. Corn is one of the best malt adjuncts available. The starches therein are easily converted to corn sugar. Corn can be used in many forms from the basic kernel to cornmeal. It must be cooked until the mixture achieves the consistency of a gelatinized mass before adding to the mash. The usual proportions are 1 part corn to 2 parts pale malt. This mixture results in the most efficient utilization of the enzymes in the malt for starch to sugar conversion.

Rice

Rice may also be used as an adjunct by itself or in conjunction with corn (Fig. 3-6). While rice does not contain as much starch and thus as much convertible sugar as corn, it has an almost neutral flavor. It is therefore suitable for very pale beers. Probably the best and most available rice for brewing is common brown rice. You can buy it at most supermarkets and health food stores. Some experts feel that rice imparts a certain crispness to light beer. It is used in Budweiser (Fig. 3-7).

Oats and Wheat

Oats and wheat can be used in brewing beer, but their value to you is not significant enough to warrant detail here. A few beers and ales are brewed with other grains, but the procedures necessary for success are quite detailed.

When buying malted barley grain for brewing, look at the overall condition of the grain you are considering purchasing. There should be very little dust, foreign matter, or debris. A high quantity of straw or other material in the grain indicates that the quality of the grain is questionable.

Inspecting Grains

The grains should be plump and all of about equal length and shape. Pale malt should be close to straw in color.

Fig. 3-6. Rice is also a malt adjunct.

Fig. 3-7. Budweiser beer uses rice.

Look at a few individual grains. Each one should crush easily between your fingers and have a powdery center. One test of quality malted barley grain is that you should be able to write with a broken piece, much the same as you could with chalk. Beware of any grain that you cannot personally check. If you are dealing with a reputable store, examining the malted barley before sale should be possible. Ask questions if you are in doubt. The more you know about ingredients—such as origin, age, etc.—the better educated you will be at brewing.

Purchase just enough grain to brew one batch of beer. If you are satisfied with the results, buy as much as your pocketbook will allow. The keeping quality of good malted barley is excellent providing the grain is stored properly (Fig. 3-8).

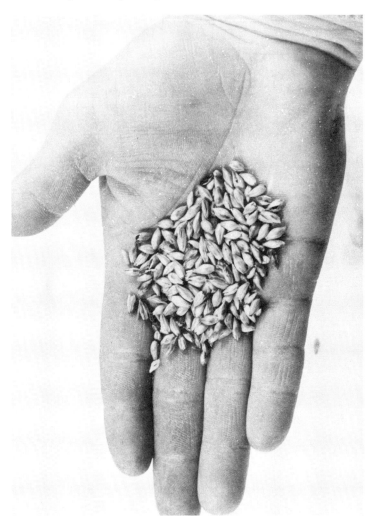

Fig. 3-8. Barley grains.

Fig. 3-9. Leaf hops.

HOPS

The value of hops in beer is often underestimated, especially by those of us who have been drinking American beer for most of our lives. Most of our domestic beers are very lightly hopped. When we taste a beer that has a lot of flavor such as Heineken, we often find the new taste very appealing. When we brew our own beer, we need to try different types of hops, both imported and domestic, before we can really learn which types are best (Fig. 3-9).

Hops were not used in brewing beer until around the fourteenth century. Before then, plants used for flavoring included *pennyroyal, balsam, juniper, mint, tansy, wormwood, betony,* and even fresh hay. In your advanced brewing stage, you may want to try some of these other plants instead of hops.

The hops used in modern brewing are one of the fastest growing plants on earth. Each vine is capable of growing as much as 1 foot in height per day under ideal soil, water, and sunlight conditions.

Humulus lupulus (hop plant) grows almost anywhere in the world where the conditions are right. I have discovered growths of hops in many areas of North America and have tried these for brewing beer at home. The time for harvesting hops—only the female buds are used for brewing—is crucial to success. The chances of finding suitable wild hops and picking them at the right time are remote. Nevertheless, if you know where wild hops grow and can harvest them at the right time (in England, all hops are harvested within a day or two of September 6), you can realize a substantial savings in beer making ingredients.

Commercially Grown Hops

In most cases your best choice will be one or more of the commercially grown hops. There are many types grown in North America, England, and Europe. The United States is second only to Germany in annual production of hops for brewing.

Hops are grown commercially by training the vines to grow up strings or wires. The plants spiral upward to as high as 30 feet. The hop plant is *dioecious*, which means that there are separate male and female plants. One male plant can fertilize around 500 female plants. Some feel that a fertilized female does not offer the best quality hops for brewing. For this reason, male plants are unwanted. They are almost impossible to eliminate totally as they grow wild all around the world. In continental Europe the male hop plant has been outlawed for hundreds of years.

The hops used in the brewing process, both commercial and on the home front, are the cone-shaped flowers of the female plant. Each flower consists of from 50 to 100 petals. Female hop flowers are harvested when ripe, dried, pressed, and often ground and finally molded into pellets.

All of the commercially grown hops available for sale to the home brewer generally are of good quality. The main differences are related to the aroma and strength of individual samples. Some popular and reliable brands are Cascade, Hallertauer, Fuggles, and Saaz. These brands are available in either the leaf form or pellets. In the beginning stages of brewing, it is probably safe to stick with the pelletized types. Try the leaf varieties as you master the basic brewing skills.

Leaf Hops

Unless care is exercised in handling and storing leaf hops, they will lose much of their flavor and aroma. Smell hops to determine their freshness. Hops that are old will not have much aroma. They will be of little value in brewing unless you use great handfuls. American commercial brewers use about 3 ounces of dried hops per barrel of beer. Most hops sold today are sealed in plastic or foil packages. This prevents the sniff test, but these hops should be of good quality.

Look at the overall condition and color of the flowers. Fresh hops of good quality should be bright green to gold, depending on type. Dull, brownish colors indicate that the hops are not the best of the harvest and will not offer the best hop flavor.

Good hops will not contain foreign matter such as stems, dirt, or seeds. Because seeds indicate that the hop plant has been fertilized by a male plant, some experts feel that seeded hops are of inferior quality. Run your own tests to see if seeds do reduce the overall quality of hops. A few British varieties of the hops contain seeds. The growers feel that once a female hop plant has been fertilized, the plant ripens more quickly and develops more fully.

Finishing Hops

Hops are probably the most costly beer ingredient, but it is false economy to skimp on quality. In time you will learn that one type of hop is ideal for adding to the wort, but it is not worth much as a finishing hop. Other brands of hops are finishing hops. Finishing hops are either leaf or pellet hops that are added to the boiling wort during the last 5 to 10 minutes of boiling. These hops are used to simply add a bit more flavor, and usually they are of a particular type such as Fuggles or Kent (Fig. 3-10).

YEAST

Beer, ale, and wine would all be nonalcoholic beverages if not for yeast. The ability of the yeast organisms to convert sugar into alcohol is what gives these beverages their zip. No one really knows who first discovered that yeast will convert sugar to alcohol, but yeast was being used around 1400 B.C.

Top-Fermenting and Bottom-Fermenting Yeasts

There are many types of yeast organisms, but you only need to be concerned with bottom-fermenting and top-fermenting yeasts. Bottom-fermenting yeasts are only used for brewing beer. Top-fermenting yeasts are used primarily for brewing ale. These yeasts are different from bakers' yeast, although they have the same scientific name—*Saccharomyces cerevisiae*. Bakers' yeast is a special strain that will not settle out properly from your brew (Fig. 3-11). It is used for making bread.

Fig. 3-10. Pellet hops.

Fig. 3-11. Baker's yeast should never be used for brewing beer.

Beer made with bakers' yeast will have a heavy yeast taste and will almost surely be cloudy. A bakers' yeast brew may give you heartburn if you drink it.

Another misconception about brewing beer at home is that you can use airborne yeast or yeast that may be naturally obtained from mashing the grain used in the brewing process. Brewer's yeast tablets are not an active yeast culture and are useless for brewing beer.

Pick a bottom-fermenting yeast for lager beers and a top-fermenting yeast for ale or stout. Pure yeast strains of both are readily available from beer making supply stores and through mail-order suppliers (Fig. 3-12).

Reusing Yeast

Good yeast cultures can be used repeatedly. Some commercial breweries have used the same basic yeast culture for more than 30 years with excellent success. One advantage of reusing yeast is reduced costs, simply because you do not have to buy additional yeast for every batch of beer. Another advantage of using the same yeast is that the taste of the beer will be very similar in all batches, assuming that other ingredients and factors remain equal.

If you would like to reuse yeast, remember that when it is first pitched into the primary fermenter and begins to convert the sugars into alcohol and esters, the yeast will increase in mass by about 30 percent. At the end of the primary fermentation stage (about three to five days), almost all the yeast will have settled to the bottom of the fermentation tank. You will reclaim your yeast from this settling but you must be very careful in your approach.

Sediment on the bottom of the primary fermentation tank consists of dead yeast organisms, hop residues, and live yeast cultures. The only things of value to you are the organisms that lie in a layer at approximately the middle of the sediment. After you have siphoned off the beer into the secondary fermenter, you must carefully scrape off the top layer of the sediment. A wooden spoon works well. Work in the center of the mass and carefully spoon out about 2 tablespoonsful of the active yeast culture. This yeast will be light in color and clean looking. Place the yeast on a paper towel to drain for a few minutes. Either pitch it directly into your next batch of beer wort or save it for later use in your freezer.

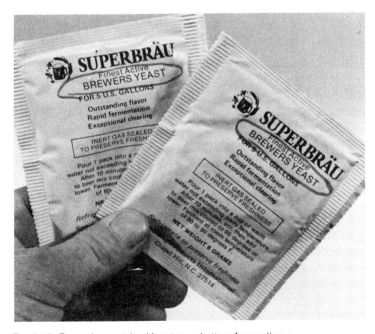

Fig. 3-12. Brewer's yeast is either top or bottom fermenting.

Yeast should be reused as soon as possible. Your best results will be achieved if the yeast is pitched directly into another batch of beer. If this is not possible, however, you can freeze the yeast as follows. After draining the yeast culture, wrap it in a sheet of plastic wrap. Seal in a small plastic or glass container. Place it in your freezer until needed. Before using, let the yeast thaw to room temperature and then place it in a starter bottle—malt extract and water solution that activates the yeast. After the yeast is working well (usually within one day), pitch it into the beer wort.

If you are thinking about trying to recycle or reuse yeast, another technique may be worthwhile and less complicated. Because the beer in a primary fermenter contains active yeast cultures, you can use these to start another batch of beer. Simply take about 1 cup of the liquid from a working batch of beer. Pitch this into a freshly made wort. The active yeast cultures from one batch will go to work on the sugar in the second batch. This technique assumes that you are continually making beer.

Another method you can use to reclaim active yeast cultures involves using beer that has not been pasteurized at the commercial brewery. This rules out canned or bottled beer; with few exceptions, all beer in these containers has been pasteurized. One possibility is to buy a pint or quart of beer from a tavern that sells draft beer. Take this unpasteurized beer home and pitch it into a wort. Draft beer contains active yeast cultures that should start to work on the sugars in your wort. If no activity is apparent after two days, simply add a package of brewer's yeast. If you see signs of yeast activity within a day or so, you can safely assume that you have obtained good yeast. One advantage of this technique is that you will be obtaining a very specialized yeast indirectly from a commercial brewery.

SUGAR

Many beer and ale recipes in this book require that sugar be

Fig. 3-13. Corn sugar is the best type of sugar for brewing beer at home.

added to the wort. The addition of sugar is an inexpensive way of providing food for the yeast culture, which in turn converts these sugars into alcohol. Sugar tends to make a beer lighter than if it is brewed solely from grain. Sugar also speeds up the brewing process.

When barley grain is malted, one of the by-products is *maltose* or malt sugar. If beer is being brewed from malt extract syrup, the amount of available sugar will be lower than if the actual barley grains (and adjuncts such as corn) are used. To compensate for the lower sugar content, you can add sugar to the wort before putting the mixture in the primary fermenter. Small amounts of sugar are again added just prior to bottling.

Corn sugar, which is commonly available at any shop selling beer and wine making supplies, is the best type of sugar for the home brewer. Corn sugar (also called *dextrose*) is most easily fermentable when compared with other sugars (Fig. 3-13).

Sugar (sucrose) is frequently used by home brewers with sad results. While this white table sugar is found in practically

73

every American home, it will not produce a beer that can be considered fine, except regarding alcoholic content, which will be about the same as that produced by corn sugar. Sucrose is not as readily fermentable as dextrose. The end result is a beer that tends to be cidery or slightly sour. Nevertheless, many home brewers use cane sugar and have grown accustomed to the taste. You may certainly experiment with cane sugar in granulated or powder form, but remember that you may produce beer that will have a cidery taste.

Honey can sometimes be used to good advantage when brewing beer or, more properly, mead. Mead is one brew that you will probably want to try as you become more proficient at brewing. The main problem with using honey in brewing is cost. Pound for pound, honey is about four times as expensive as corn sugar (Fig. 3-14).

You may want to use *lactose* or milk sugar and even artificial sweeteners in your brewing. My only advice is don't. While lactose can be used for special brews—milk stout, for

Fig. 3-14. Honey is sometimes used for brewing mead.

example—this sugar is unfermentable by brewing yeast. It will therefore not be converted to alcohol. Lactose is used for sweetening and not for yeast conversion. It is therefore a poor choice for the home brewer. The same is true for artificial sweeteners.

BREWING ADDITIVES AND AIDS

Finings or fining agents are commonly added to beer and ale to make them more clear than they are at the time of bottling. Beer that is properly made and allowed to sit undisturbed will be very clear. This process takes about six to eight weeks. You may want to speed up the clarification process (which will occur normally over time) by adding some type of fining agent.

Gelatin

There are two ways to clarify beer. The first method is to add dissolved gelatin to the brew about one to two days before bottling. While special gelatins are available from beer and wine supply stores, you can do just as well with the unflavored gelatins sold in most supermarkets. Mix one package (about 1 ounce) in about 1 cup of warm water until completely dissolved. Simply lift off the air lock on the secondary fermenter, add the gelatin, stir to disperse evenly, then replace the air lock. Allow the gelatin to work for at least 24 hours, then bottle the beer in the usual manner. The gelatin will settle to the bottom of the secondary fermenter. It will carry almost all the yeast and protein particles with it. The end result will be a very clear beer.

Isinglass Finings

Isinglass finings may be used to clarify beer. These are available from beer and wine supply stores (along with other types of finings). Isinglass is a semitransparent gelatin prepared from the air bladders of sturgeons. Isinglass is added to the brew a day or so before bottling. This neutralizes any electrical charge in the yeast and protein particles in the beer. The isinglass and particulate matter in the brew settle to the bottom of the secondary fermenter.

Gypsum, Bentonite, and Raw Egg Whites

Other fining agent powders such as gypsum and *bentonite* (a natural clay fining) are available. One other method, which I have never tried, is to use raw egg whites. Raw egg whites as explained to me by an experienced brewer of excellent beers, will clarify a 5-gallon batch of beer in about three hours. Simply drop the whites from four eggs into the secondary fermenter, stir a few times, then allow liquid to settle for several hours. Bottling is then done in the usual manner.

Heading Powder or Liquid

Under normal brewing conditions, almost every beer will produce a natural head when poured into a glass container. If you find that your beer lacks a thick creamy head, you may want to add a *heading powder* (difficult to use) or heading liquid (easier to use) prior to bottling your beer.

Yeast Nutrient Powder

Yeast nutrient powder can be used if you discover that the yeast is a little weak. The actions of yeast cultures should be very apparent within 24 hours after the yeast is added. If this is not the case, you can often recharge the yeast by adding yeast nutrient powder. Under normal conditions, however, yeast nutrient powder should not be required. Yeast nutrient powder is handy when you are recycling yeast cultures from one batch to another.

Beechwood Curls

Beechwood curls or wood chips are used to give your beer a beechwood flavor similar to that of Budweiser. The wood chips are sterilized in boiling water before use. They are simply dumped into the secondary fermenter at the same time the beer is siphoned into this container. The secondary fermenter is then sealed with an air lock and allowed to settle for around 10 days. The theory behind the beechwood chips is that they impart a special flavor in the beer.

Sodium Metabisulfite

Sodium metabisulfite is mainly used as a sterilizing agent for cleaning brewing equipment and bottles. It can also be used as a preservative in beer to prevent spoilage. It is the only preservative allowed in beers and ales made in Great Britain. Sodium metabisulfite is available at beer and wine supply shops (Fig. 3-15).

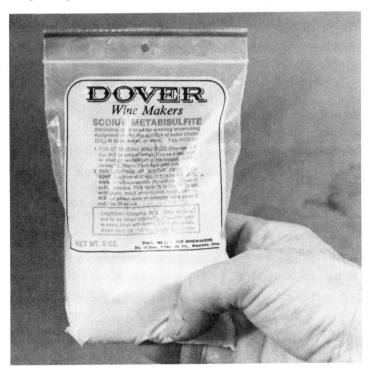

Fig. 3-15. Sodium metabisulfite is a good sterilizing agent when mixed properly in water.

Ascorbic Acid

Ascorbic acid can be used at bottling time as a preservative in the same manner as sodium metabisulfite. Some experts claim that adding this acid in beer prevents bitterness by prohibiting the deterioration of the hop particles suspended in the beer.

Campden Tablets

Campden tablets are made from sodium bisulfite and must be crushed and dissolved before use. This powder contains sulfur dioxide that kills wild yeast and bacteria—good sources of infection for your brew. It can also be used for sterilizing brewing equipment and bottles. The chemical is also available in granular form, which works better and is cheaper than the campden tablets.

Chlorine Bleach

Chlorine bleach is the strongest sterilizing agent available to you. Use bleach when you are cleaning really dirty or contaminated equipment and bottles. A 10 percent solution is most effective. Simply mix 2 fluid ounces of household bleach in 1 pint of water. At this strength, the chlorine solution will kill any wild yeast and bacteria. After soaking the equipment in this solution for about 10 minutes, rinse several times in running water to remove all traces of the chlorine. Equipment not thoroughly rinsed will result in your beer tasting like it was made with swimming pool water.

If you use the chlorine bleach wash for equipment, you can neutralize the chlorine, after it has soaked for a few minutes, by washing the equipment again in a 10 percent solution of sodium metabisulfite. Because sodium metabisulfite produces sulfur dioxide, which is a chemical that is incompatible with chlorine, the two will neutralize each other.

Burton Water Salts

Burton water salts increase the pH of the water used in brewing. Burton water salts are a blend of natural minerals that react with the malt extract and condition the water. The minerals in the salts react under low temperatures (around 40 degrees Fahrenheit) with proteins and yeast in the beer to prevent cloudiness.

Licorice Sticks

Licorice sticks are a natural additive that is sometimes used in special medicinal stouts. This black substance comes from the root of the licorice plant herb, and it produces a distinct taste and aroma. The black oily sticks are dissolved in warm water and then added to the brew in the secondary fermenter where the taste will permeate the liquid.

Tincture of Iodine

Tincture of iodine is used to test for starch in mashed barley grain prior to brewing. Begin by removing about 1 teaspoon of the mashed grain liquor from the mash tun. Place it on a white (clean) saucer or dish. Add a few drops of tincture of iodine to the liquor. The brown iodine will turn a deep bluish-black color almost immediately if starch is present. A high proportion of blackish grains usually indicates that the grain was not crushed sufficiently. The sample is discarded after testing, and all equipment is sterilized before reuse. No reaction between the liquor and tincture of iodine is a good indication that there is no starch present.

Brewing Beer

Before you can begin brewing beer for the first time, you must buy the needed ingredients. I would suggest the following: 1 can unhopped malt extract syrup, 5 pounds corn sugar, 1 package brewer's yeast, and 1 packet of hop pellets.

Buy the least expensive can of unhopped malt extract syrup you can find. Blue Ribbon malt extract syrup will probably be available again by the time this book is published. It is currently off the market; production was stopped in late 1981. Home brewers mostly have had imported malt extract syrups from which to choose. Imported malt syrup is almost twice the price of that produced in this country.

The other ingredients are readily available. Choose fresh ingredients especially in the case of yeast and hops. It is hard to go wrong, however, as packaged brewer's yeast (10 grams) and hop pellets have a long shelf life.

I would recommend any of the fine hops from the Northwest. These are commonly referred to as *Cascade hops* (Fig. 4-1). They are available from any beer and wine making supply store or through the mail. The pellet type is of good quality

Fig. 4-1. Cascade hops are popular among home brewers.

and keeps well for long periods. This type is generally cheaper than the imported varieties.

MATERIALS

You also need a ⅜-inch diameter, 6-foot length clear plastic hose for siphoning, a hydrometer (for checking the specific gravity of your beer during brewing), a fermentation lock with stopper, and fermentation vessels (unless you already have 5-gallon carboy glass bottles or a sealable 5-gallon plastic jug). You should also buy a sterilizing agent such as campden tablets, powdered sodium metabisulfite, or sodium bisulfite. A large pot for boiling the wort, a thermometer, and a strainer are also needed.

The last batch of equipment required includes a bottle capper, bottle caps, and bottles. You will not need these items until the beer is ready to bottle—in about 10 days—so you can delay purchasing them until needed. You will need enough empties for about 5 gallons of beer—60 12-ounce bottles.

SANITATION

Before you can brew drinkable beer, you must first sterilize the equipment you will be using for the particular operation in which you are engaged. When starting a batch of beer, you will need a 5-gallon primary fermenter, a large cooking pot that holds at least 2 gallons, a siphon hose, and a large wooden spoon for stirring the wort.

Begin by washing the cooking pot in a sterilizing solution (2 teaspoons sterilizing agent in 2 gallons of warm water) (Fig. 4-2). Let the pot soak for a few minutes, then pour the solution

Fig. 4-2. Sterilize your equipment and bottles with a sodium metabisulfite solution.

Fig. 4-3. Malt extract syrup is simple to use.

into the primary fermenter and let it soak for a time. Rinse the cooking pot out well with fresh water.

Put about 1 gallon of water into the cooking pot and set it on the stove to boil. Place the unopened can of unhopped malt extract syrup in warm water. This makes it easier to pour the normally thick liquid. When the water comes to a rolling boil, remove it from the heat and add the unhopped malt extract syrup. Stir this into the water. The main reason for removing the boiling water from the stove is that undissolved malt syrup, lying in the bottom of the pot, would burn (Fig. 4-3).

After the unhopped malt extract syrup has been dissolved in the water, add 4 cups of corn sugar. Stir to dissolve the sugar. Place the pot back on the burner and bring to a boil once again. Dump in one package of hop pellets and stir into the liquid (Figs. 4-4 and 4-5).

As the liquor reaches a boil, a foam develops that tends to rise to the top of the pot. Watch for this and lower the heat as the

Fig. 4-4. Add sugar and stir until it dissolves before reheating to a boil.

Fig. 4-5. Hop pellets are dumped into the boiling wort.

foam starts to rise. Once the foam has risen, it will not do so again. Instead, it will boil.

The wort should boil for 10 minutes. As the liquor cooks, dump the contents of one yeast package into a cup of warm water. A temperature of 70 degrees Fahrenheit is ideal. You can also add about 1 teaspoon of corn sugar to this yeast starting solution. Let the yeast sit undisturbed until needed (Fig. 4-6).

Rinse out the primary fermenter. Once it has been sterilized and rinsed thoroughly, poor in about 3 gallons of cold, clean water.

After the wort has boiled for 10 minutes, remove it from the heat. Pour the wort into the primary fermenter. A wide funnel will make this task easier. Because the object is to pour only clear wort into the fermenter, you should pour the wort through cheesecloth. This will filter out almost all the hop residue. Change the cheesecloth after about every gallon of wort has been poured. Cheesecloth is a good filtering medium, but it will clog easily. Replace the cloth often.

Some experts believe it is unnecessary to filter the wort prior to going into the primary fermenter. The theory is that almost all the solids in the wort will settle out in a few days, so filtering is a wasted effort. The wort becomes slightly bitter if the bulk of the hops is left in, and this is why I recommended straining the wort. Remember that the beer will be lighter hopped if filtered.

After all the liquor has been added to the primary fermenter, add enough additional water to make 5 gallons. Then check

Fig. 4-6. Start the yeast culture in warm, sugar water before pitching into the primary fermenter.

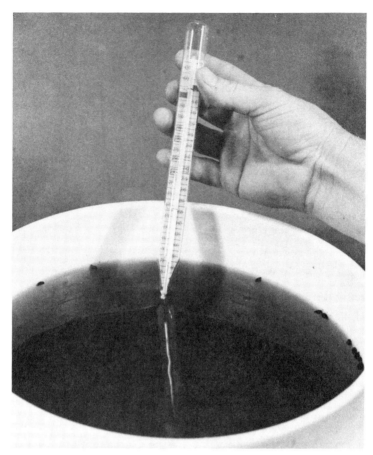

Fig. 4-7. Check the temperature of the wort before adding yeast. Add yeast when the temperature is from 70 to 80 degrees Fahrenheit.

the temperature of the wort. The wort must be around 70 degrees Fahrenheit when you add the yeast cultures (Fig. 4-7).

When the water temperature is within acceptable limits (plus or minus 70 degrees Fahrenheit), add the yeast culture that has been in the starter bottle. Stir the yeast into the wort. Cover the container. It is not necessary to seal the primary fermenter with an air lock. The wort will produce a layer of carbon dioxide that will be on top of the liquid. The container

Fig. 4-8. The started yeast culture is pitched into the wort.

must be covered to prevent the carbon dioxide from escaping (Figs. 4-8 and 4-9).

Before you cover the primary fermenter, take a sample of the liquor and test it with your hydrometer. Enter this figure in your brewer's logbook.

You should notice vigorous activity in the primary fermenter

Fig. 4-9. Cover the primary fermenter to exclude the air.

Fig. 4-10. A pancakelike layer of foam on the surface of the wort after a few hours. Fermentation is taking place.

within a 12-hour period. There will be a layer of foam on top of the wort (Fig. 4-10). The top of the container will bulge upward slightly. This activity will be steady for about two to three days. Then the foam will begin to subside. When this happens, transfer the contents of the primary fermenter into the secondary fermenter.

Clean and sterilize the secondary fermenter by scrubbing the interior with a long-handled bottle brush. Soak it in a sterilizing solution for a few minutes. After soaking, rinse the secondary fermenter several times with fresh warm water. At this time you should run some sterilizing solution through the siphon hose. Rinse with clear water.

At least one hour before transferring the contents of the primary fermenter into the secondary fermenter, place the primary fermenter on a table or kitchen counter so it will be above the secondary fermenter. The liquor then will have a chance to settle after moving.

SIPHONING
Remove the lid from the primary fermenter, then insert the

Fig. 4-11. Siphoning wort into the secondary fermenter. Work carefully to leave sediment in the primary fermenter.

Fig. 4-12. Twist the siphon hose (inflow end) so you can clearly see what is being sucked into it.

siphon hose into the liquor. Lower the tip of the siphon hose about 4 inches below the surface. Start siphoning by gently sucking on the far end of the hose. The liquor will start to flow through the clear plastic hose. Stick the outflow end into the secondary fermenter. The brew must not splash into the secondary fermenter, so place the end of the hose on the bottom of the secondary fermenter (Fig. 4-11).

While siphoning, do not disturb the liquor in the primary fermenter with the inflow end of the hose. Begin siphoning about 4 inches down from the surface. As the level drops, lower the hose to keep the end about the same distance. To aid you in seeing exactly where the inflow end of the hose is located, twist the hose slightly (Fig. 4-12). The end should appear on the side of the primary fermenter. If the primary fermenter is made from either glass or semitransparent material such as plastic, you can easily see the end of the hose. If the fermenter is of dark or solid plastic such as a trash container, you cannot see the end of the hose. In the latter case, use your best judgment to keep the inflow end of the hose off the container's bottom.

Never drop the inflow end of the siphon hose to the bottom of the primary fermenter. This causes sediment to be drawn into the hose. Tiny bits of sediment will flow from one container to another, but try to keep this to an absolute minimum. Any action that will cause the contents of the primary fermenter to become agitated, such as moving the container while siphoning, should be avoided.

When you get to the last few inches of liquor in the primary fermenter, watch the liquid that is being sucked up by the hose. When sediment begins to flow into the tube, stop siphoning. Because this sediment will not improve the beer's quality, it should be discarded (Fig. 4-13).

SECONDARY FERMENTATION

While transferring the beer from the primary fermenter to the secondary fermenter, take a sample of the liquor for

Fig. 4-13. Discard the sediment in the primary fermenter.

testing with your hydrometer. Record this figure in your brewer's logbook (Fig. 4-14).

After all the clear beer has been transferred from the primary fermenter to the secondary fermenter, install a fermentation lock or air lock in the top of the secondary fermenter. Wet the rubber stopper with a little water to ensure a tight seal. The secondary fermenter must sit undisturbed for about one week (Fig. 4-15).

The air lock will bubble during secondary fermentation. At first there will be several bubbles per minute. As fermentation becomes complete, the bubbling will slow to about one bubble every minute or two.

After about seven days, almost all bubbling in the air lock will have stopped. While this is a fairly reliable indication that the beer is ready to be bottled, use your hydrometer for a more precise determination. Beer is ready to be bottled when the liquor has reached a specific gravity of at least 1.004.

The contents of the secondary fermenter must not come in contact with the atmosphere. At the beginning of secondary

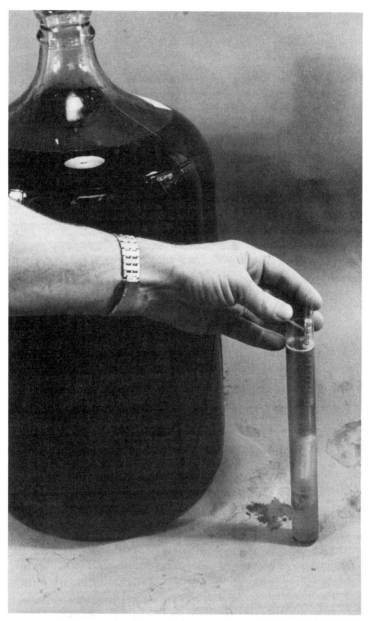

Fig. 4-14. Take a hydrometer reading as the wort is transferred from the primary fermenter to the secondary fermenter.

Fig. 4-15. Install an air lock on top of the secondary fermenter.

fermentation, the beer will give off large quantities of carbon dioxide, which acts as a shield against the atmosphere. Nevertheless, a fermentation lock should be in place. You will notice activity in the air lock at first. As the beer ferments, this action will slow and may even stop in cold weather. This is normal. As the beer ferments, less gas will be given off. The need for a fermentation lock becomes greater.

The fermenter must be covered during secondary fermentation to exclude light. I wrap my secondary fermenter in an old cloth coat. This keeps the temperature of the secondary fermenter's contents more constant (Fig. 4-16).

To help sediment settlement during secondary fermentation without the use of special additives such as gypsum, you can give the carboy a quick twist. This action helps to free sediment that often clings to the side of the container and causes it to drift downward. Do not disturb the beer in the secondary fermenter for a few hours directly before bottling. This may mean moving the secondary fermenter to a new and high location on the morning of the day that you plan to bottle your beer. Siphoning will be much easier. By moving the secondary fermenter several hours before bottling, the batch will have time to settle.

BOTTLING

Before you can start filling bottles, each must be inspected, cleaned, and sterilized. Even if you are using only quart bottles, this will take some time to do properly. Begin by assembling enough bottles in an area where they can be cleaned—probably the kitchen. Carefully inspect each bottle by holding it up to the light and looking inside through the neck. Look for any deposits, mildew, or other residue inside the bottle. Set particularly dirty bottles in the sink to soak. If you rinse beer bottles out immediately with clear water after use, you will greatly reduce the amount of cleaning needed before the bottle is refilled.

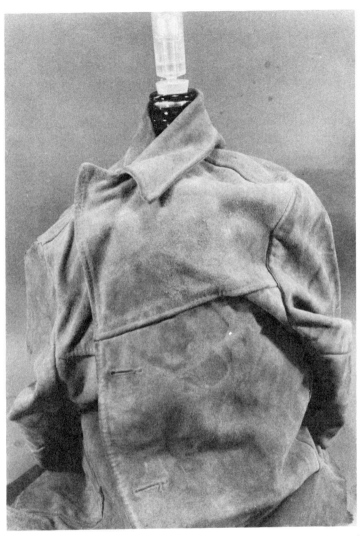

Fig. 4-16. Cover the secondary fermenter to exclude light during this stage of fermentation.

Rinse each bottle carefully with clear, warm water. Place the bottles in a large container to soak in a sterilizing solution. A good sterilizing solution can be made from dissolving 2 teaspoons of sodium bisulfite (or sodium metabisulfite) to each quart of water. A gallon of this sterilizing solution should be more than enough. Let some bottles soak in this solution for a few minutes. Rinse each bottle with hot water and set them in a kitchen drain rack to drain and dry.

Bottles that are heavily soiled or contain dried deposits inside will require more work. Use a good bottle brush to remove the internal residue. In most cases this brush will clean the inside well. For very dirty bottles, you may want to make a special sterilizing solution by mixing 2 tablespoons of common household bleach in 2 quarts of water. Pour this solution into the bottles and let it work for about five minutes. Rinse the bottles to remove all traces of the solution. Failure to remove all traces of the bleach will make your beer taste like it was made from swimming pool water. A sterilizing solution of sodium metabisulfite or sodium bisulfite will neutralize household bleach. By rinsing bottles soaked in bleach in this second solution, they will be sterilized and will not contain any off-flavors for your beer.

After the bottles have been inspected, sterilized, and rinsed in clean water, turn your attention to the siphon hose and 5-gallon container that will be used. Because the beer will be transferred from the secondary fermenter into another 5-gallon container before bottling, this container must be cleaned and sterilized, too. I prefer to transfer the beer before bottling because the sediment content will be less than if the beer was bottled directly from the secondary fermenter. A 5-gallon container with a small opening at the top will minimize exposure to the atmosphere.

After all the bottling equipment has been cleaned, gather everything together in your bottling area. You will also need a bottle capper, bottle caps, and a sugar priming solution. I like to soak my caps in a container of hot water before using, and you might want to do the same (Fig. 4-17).

A sugar priming solution is used to help carbonate the beer and give it a healthy head when poured. This addition will start fermentation in the bottles. To make a sugar priming solution, simply dissolve 1 to 1.25 cups of corn sugar in 1 cup of boiling water. This solution will be added to the 5 gallons of beer just prior to bottling (Fig. 4-18).

An alternate method of priming your beer is to add 1 teaspoon of corn sugar to each quart bottle before filling. This method requires a lot more work than bulk priming; each bottle is primed individually. Nevertheless, some home brewers like this method better than bulk priming. If you decide to use this method, a small funnel is very helpful. The priming sugar will not stick to the neck of dry bottles (Fig. 4-19).

Assemble your equipment in the most advantageous arrangement. The 5-gallon beer container should be up high so it will siphon well. Locate the bottle caps within reach of the capper.

Begin by siphoning the beer from the secondary fermenter into the 5-gallon container. Suck up as little sediment as possible. When you have almost drained the secondary fermenter, stop siphoning. Place the 5 gallons of beer up higher than the work area. Stir the sugar priming solution into the beer if you are bulk priming. Because you have carefully siphoned only the clear beer, from the secondary fermenter, you need not worry about stirring up sediment in the beer.

Begin the siphoning action in the hose and start filling the empty bottles. Stick the outflow end of the hose down into the

Fig. 4-17. Soak crown caps in warm water prior to use.

Fig. 4-18. To bulk prime, first dissolve 1 cup of corn sugar in 1 cup of boiling water.

bottom of each bottle so that the beer will not splash. Each bottle is filled up to about 1.5 inches from the top. The flow is cut off by pressing the special control clip (Fig. 4-20).

By working with a shutoff clip on the siphon hose, you will

have a lot of control. You will greatly reduce the chances of spilling beer while filling bottles. You will be able to shut off the flow of beer at just the right moment. Place a cap on each bottle and set them next to the capper. The edges of the crown cap are crimped downward to seal.

Fig. 4-19. Instead of bulk priming, you can add up to 2 teaspoonsful of corn sugar to each quart bottle before filling with beer.

Fig. 4-20. A flow shutoff clip is very handy when filling bottles with siphon hose.

Fig. 4-21. Set up your capping operation for a smooth work flow from left to right.

When capping filled beer bottles, the work will progress much easier if it is set up according to your needs. Locate the filled but uncapped bottles to the left of the capping machine. Assuming you are right-handed, the work flow will be from left to right. Pick up a filled bottle, place it in the capping machine, crimp the cap in place, then remove the capped bottle to the right (Fig. 4-21).

As the bottles are capped, move them to the right and, ideally, into carrying cases or storage cases. Having the bottles of beer in one box or carton will make handling and moving much easier than moving a few at a time.

After all the beer has been bottled, you should store it for several weeks to allow it to age properly. Storage and aging are covered in Chapter 5.

After bottling, you must clean all utensils and equipment. Ideally you will immediately start another batch of beer, thus keeping your equipment in use.

The variety of beers that can be produced by using canned

malt extract syrup is limited only to the available ingredients. In Chapter 6 you will find recipes calling for particular types of malt extract syrup and different combinations (and types) of hops.

MASHING GRAINS

The main difference between brewing beer from whole grains (barley) and canned malt extract is that it is possible to achieve a finer beer with grains. Another reason for using whole grains in the brewing process is that you can produce more kinds of beer simply by varying the type of barley used. The basic brewing procedures covered earlier still apply when using whole grains. Chapter 3 discusses the malting of barley grains.

After the barley grains have been malted, the next step in producing an all-grain beer is to mash the grains. The mashing process, when carried out on a commercial level, is a rather massive task that involves very large volumes of grain. You will work with only small amounts. There are four steps: treating the water, grinding the grain, cooking the malt (actually mashing), and sparging.

When brewing beer at home using canned malt extract syrup, the water you use will be straight out of the tap. Unless your water is especially hard or soft, the results will be totally acceptable. When you think in terms of mashing whole grains, the quality of the water becomes much more important.

pH of Water

The hardness or softness (acid or alkaline, respectively) is expressed as pH, which is simply a measurement scale. The pH scale goes from 0.0 to 14.0, with a pH of 7.0 considered neutral.

Water with a pH of around 5.0 (on the acid side of the scale) is the best for mashing whole grain. Test and adjust the pH of the water you will be using for mashing your barley malt.

Have a sample of your water analyzed by the local public water supply company. You will receive an evaluation of your water and a pH value. It is generally a simple matter of adjusting your water so that it will have a lower pH number, which means slightly acidic. The most common way of lowering the pH of your water is to add Burton water salts.

If you live in the country and your water comes from a well, you should still have the water analyzed to determine the pH. Several water testing kits are on the market that you can use to determine the pH of your water. Some of these kits are nothing more than special test strips (slips of specially treated paper) that will turn various colors when they are dipped in the water.

Your brewing water should be rated as to hardness at around 450 parts per million (ppm) for the best grain mashing results. One teaspoonful of Burton water salts added to 5 gallons of water will increase the overall hardness (acidity) by approximately 150 ppm. If your water is rated at about 75 ppm (neutral), add 2.5 teaspoons of Burton water salts to arrive at the best overall pH of the water you will be using for mashing (5 gallons). Four-hundred-fifty less 75 equals 375 ppm. At 150 ppm per teaspoon you will need 2.5 teaspoonsful of Burton water salts to increase water hardness from 75 ppm to 450 ppm.

Crushing Barley Malt

After you have adjusted the pH of 5 gallons of water, you can crush the barley malt. The key here is to convert the whole grain into a coarsely ground mass. Texture of the crushed grain is very important to success in mashing. Grain that is not crushed sufficiently will not have enough starches exposed to the enzymes to produce the desired malt extract.

Conversely, if the grain is ground too much (pulverized, for example), the malt will be difficult or impossible to strain out completely when the mashing has been completed. The proper texture of grain for mashing is described as mealy, where every grain of the malt has been broken up.

You can use a blender or food processor to crush malt. Place .5 to 1 cup of whole grain into the blender. Turn the machine on and off rapidly several times until the grain has been crushed sufficiently. If you make dust out of the grain, the resultant beer will be cloudy (when chilled) as a result of the minute particles (mainly protein) in the beer during all fermentation stages.

You may also use a kitchen meat grinder to crush whole malted barley. While slower than using the blender, this method commonly results in grain that has been crushed properly. Simply run small amounts of the grain through the grinder until the proper texture is achieved.

A rolling pin may be used to crush whole barley malt. This method is time-consuming and requires plenty of effort, but you can clearly see what is taking place. The chance of pulverizing much of the grain is eliminated. Work with small amounts of whole grain in a cookie sheet. This helps you to keep the grain in one contained area and makes dumping the crushed grain into the mash tun simple.

Look at Table 4-1 to see how much water you will need for mashing various amounts of grain. Actual amounts are listed

Table 4-1. Gallons of Mash Water Required for Various Amounts of Malted Barley.

Pounds of Grain	Gallons of Mash Water
1	1
2	1
3	1.5
4	1.5
5	2
6	2
7	2.5
8	2.5

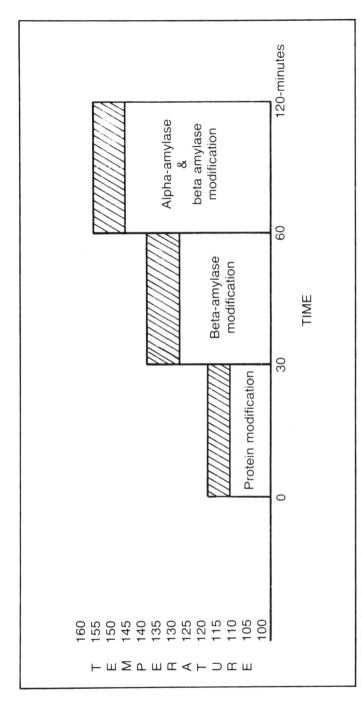

Fig. 4-22. Mashing temperature ranges.

in Chapter 6. Refer back to Table 4-1 when working with specific amounts of grain. When mashing 1 or 2 pounds of grain, you will generally use about 1 gallon of water. Use about 2 gallons of water for mashing 5 or 6 pounds of grain. Too much water in the mash tun will tend to dilute the enzymes, and too little water often leads to scorching the mash.

Heat the water up to the proper temperature, then stir in the ground malt. Figure 4-22 clearly shows that all mashing is accomplished between the temperatures of 110 to 155 degrees Fahrenheit. Heat the water to 155 degrees Fahrenheit, add the crushed malt, and stir the mixture. Cool the mixture to 110 degrees Fahrenheit. Reheat the mixture to 155 degrees Fahrenheit. Stir and allow it to cool to 110 degrees Fahrenheit again. Repeat this process for 120 minutes. At this time the starch in the mixture should be converted into sugar. Rather than relying solely on time and temperature for starch conversion, you should use the iodine starch test to determine when complete conversion has occurred.

Iodine Starch Test

The iodine starch test is a very simple procedure. Place 2 tablespoons of the liquid on a white saucer (Fig. 4-23). Put a few tincture of iodine drops in the saucer and mix with the mash. If the mixture turns bluish-purple, starch is still present in the mixture and the mashing is not complete. Continue cooking for another 10 minutes as described earlier, then retest. Continue this procedure until the test does not result in a bluish-purple color. Absence of this color means that all the starch in the mash has been converted into fermentable sugar. Pour the test mixture down your drain after testing.

Sparging

When the starch has been converted into fermentable sugar (maltose sugar), remove the mash tun from the heat. Pour the

Fig. 4-23. The iodine test will indicate the presence of starch in the mash.

mixture through a strainer and into another pot (Fig. 4-24). This liquid is now the wort, which is boiled with hops for a period and then dumped into the primary fermenter. The grain must now be rinsed several times.

Sparge the crushed barley malt by placing it in a container and adding enough boiling water to cover it (Fig. 4-25). The mixture is stirred, then poured once again through the strainer. Repeat several times until the water runs almost clear. Do not use more water than needed for the particular batch of beer you are making. Remember that the next step is to cook this liquid with hops prior to dumping into the primary fermenter.

109

Hints

A good thermometer is essential for successful mashing. Because protein modification and conversion of both alpha-amylase and beta-amylase starches happen within rather limited temperature ranges, you need to know precisely what the temperature of the mixture in the mash tun is at all times. A suitable brewing thermometer should go up to about 200 degrees Fahrenheit and ideally float, so it can be left in the mash tun at all times.

As the mash is cooking, make sure that hot spots do not develop in the mash tun. These give a burnt taste to the finished beer. To prevent overly hot spots in the mash tun, stir occasionally with a wooden spoon.

Because American malt is considered undermodified with a high amylase content, as compared to British malts that are commonly fully modified, strict temperature variations need not necessarily be followed. Some experts suggest that the crushed mash simply be cooked at 158 degrees Fahrenheit for one hour. When imported and fully modified malt is used, however, the cooking times recommended in Fig. 4-22 should

Fig. 4-24. Strain the mash to catch the grain.

Fig. 4-25. Sparging the grain to get more extract.

be followed. The hotter the mixture is during mashing, the more fixed dextrins will be produced. Fixed dextrins produce a beer with more body. The longer the cooking time of the mash, the greater the astringency of the beer and the harsher the flavors. Stout would be cooked much longer than lager or lighter beers.

If you are making a 5-gallon batch of beer and you are planning to cook the wort (with hops) for about one hour, you can start with 6 gallons of wort. When you are rinsing or sparging the mash, you can use up to 6 gallons of water. During the boiling of the wort and hops, about 1 gallon of the liquid will boil off or vaporize. The end result will be 5 gallons of beer that will be put into the primary fermenter.

You should taste the liquor during sparging of the mash. At first the liquor will be sweet. After several rinses, sweetness will diminish as the available sugars are washed out of the grain. In most cases three or four rinses will remove the maltose sugar. There is really no need to rinse again. One good way of monitoring the amount of sugar still available is to taste the liquor. When your taste buds tell you that there is little if any sugar left, you can stop sparging the mash and begin boiling the wort.

After the mash has been sparged thoroughly, the spent grains should be discarded. If you have a garden, the mash should go into the compost pile. If you have chickens or other small livestock, the spent grains make excellent feed.

Crushing of barley malt grains often poses problems for the home brewer. You should consider buying barley malt that has already been crushed by the dealer. Barley malt that has been crushed too much will be like flour. It will clog equipment and be impossible to remove. Barley malt that has not been crushed enough will be too coarse for water to enter (each grain) to extract the starch sugar.

You may save money when purchasing pale barley malt if you buy in large quantities—20 to 50-pound lots. Before buying, however, make a test batch of beer to determine the overall quality of the grain. It is not really a good idea to purchase crystal or black malt in large quantities. You will not use much of these grains in brewing.

If you buy large quantities of pale barley malt, store the grain carefully. Store the grain in an airtight container under dry conditions and a constant temperature of 50 to 60 degrees Fahrenheit.

Storing and Aging Beer

While many home brewers begin drinking beer right after it is bottled, this so-called green beer is not a quality brew. The priming sugar needs about two weeks to produce sufficient carbonation in the beer. There is also a small amount of yeast sediment that must settle to the bottom of each bottle.

The beer should be placed in a safe place with a constant temperature of between 60 to 70 degrees Fahrenheit. The bottles should be stored in cases in case they explode. This will happen if too much priming sugar has been used—either bulk priming or individually. The combination of too much priming sugar, bottling before secondary fermentation is complete, and a high ambient room temperature will result in a batch of beer that will have too much internal pressure and may explode.

After the beer has been stored undisturbed for several days, give each bottle a sharp twist. This action will help to dislodge any yeast sediment forming on the sides of the bottles and cause it to settle to the bottom.

While the beer is ready for drinking after about two weeks, it will be much better if it is allowed to age for a longer period. Most experts agree that fermentation has been completed after about six weeks, and the beer will not get any better. The beer will not start to deteriorate in quality for several years. Recently I had a chance to sample some home brew that was two years old, and it was just as good as beer that was eight weeks old. It is really doubtful, though, that you will keep home brewed beer around for such an extended period.

Beer should always be stored in a dark place. If this is not possible because of space limitations, cover the stack of beer cases with a blanket or other suitable covering. Even though most beer bottles are made from dark-colored glass, I feel that the beer should never be stored where it will be in direct sunlight. Internal pressure may increase to a dangerous level.

DEALING WITH EXPLODING BEER BOTTLES

I have never had one bottle of beer explode in almost 10 years of brewing. If you discover that your beer has too much internal pressure and the bottles are exploding, quick action is required to save the rest of the batch. Before you do anything, however, you must first protect yourself from flying glass. Put on your heaviest coat, gloves, and some type of face shield to protect your eyes. When moving cases of beer, first cover the case with a blanket or other thick material. Thus protected, the chances of flying glass are reduced dramatically.

Move the beer to a cold location. If you live in an area that experiences cold winters, simply place the beer outdoors. In the summertime you should place the beer in a refrigerator for several hours.

After the beer has cooled for several hours, remove the cap from every bottle to help reduce pressure. Recap the bottles and place them back in storage. By releasing the internal pressure inside the bottles, the chances of any more explosions should be nil. Keep checking the beer to be safe. You need not be concerned about the beer spoiling in this case. There is obviously plenty of carbon dioxide being produced internally, and the beer inside the bottles will therefore be shielded against airborne yeasts and bacteria.

If you prime and store your home brew correctly, you may never have an explosion. Problems develop when priming and bottling are approached in a carefree manner.

CHILLING AND DECANTING BEER

After your beer has aged for approximately six weeks, sample the brew and evaluate your efforts. Place a few bottles in the refrigerator to chill for several hours. The experts don't agree on the proper temperature of homemade beer, but I like mine chilled to around 45 degrees Fahrenheit. The beer will be at this temperature after two to four hours in the home refrigerator.

After the beer has been chilled, remove it from the refrigerator and carefully place it on a solid surface. Try your best not to agitate the beer, or the yeast sediment in the bottom will become suspended in the beer and make it cloudy. Carefully remove the crown cap with a bottle opener (Fig. 5-1).

The beer must be decanted or poured into another container. Remember that a small deposit of yeast is on the bottom of the beer bottle. While this yeast will not harm you in any way, it will give a yeastlike flavor to the beer and make it cloudy. The yeast is full of vitamins. Brewer's yeast, when taken internally, will cause your body to give off small amounts of carbon dioxide. Pour carefully and slowly until you see the sediment starting to flow toward the neck of the bottle. Stop pouring, dump the remainder of the beer down the drain, and rinse out the bottle.

Now you are ready to taste your first homemade beer. Fill a glass from the decanter and take a sip. The beer will not taste anything at all like commercially made beer. Your beer contains no chemicals to alter the natural taste. I think you will agree that homemade beer is far superior to store-bought beer (Fig. 5-2).

Fig. 5-1. Open home brew carefully.

Fig. 5-2. Homemade beer is a delight.

You will want to write some comments about each batch in your brewer's logbook so that you can come up with recipes that are your favorites. Consider the following: clarity of the beer, head, carbonation, taste, smell, and overall quality. Chapter 9 deals with common brewing problems. If you are dissatisfied with your home brew on one or more levels, you can correct the problem next time around.

Recipes for Beer, Ale, and Stout

There are easily thousands of different recipes for beer, ale, and stout. It is not uncommon for the home brewer to become confused. The brewer develops a standard procedure for brewing one type of beer and brews batch after batch of it. If your aim is to simply produce inexpensive, good tasting beer, you may not want to experiment with different ingredients and recipes. If you like the challenge of working with a variety of ingredients and want to discover what tastes you find most pleasing in home brew, then you will find many good recipes in this chapter.

As you may recall, there are bottom-fermented beers and top-fermented beers. This designation describes the type of yeast used in the brewing process. Bottom-fermenting yeasts are used for brewing lagers. Top-fermenting yeasts are used for brewing ales and stouts. Ales include brown beer, mild ale, pale ale, and bitter ale. Stouts include bitter, milk, and Russian. Both bottom and top-fermenting yeasts are available from beer and wine making supply stores and through mail-order companies.

If the American beer drinker limits his drinking only to bottles, cans, and draft beer, he will not find that much difference between brands. In other beer drinking countries, where the per capita consumption is much greater than our own, there are more varieties of beer, ale, and stout.

There is really only one solution to the lack of variety problem, and that is to brew your own beer. In this chapter you will find recipes for a variety of good tasting, economical beers, ales, and stouts. Follow the directions carefully and observe standard brewing practices and techniques described in Chapter 4 to ensure that your home brew comes out with predictable results.

BEERS MADE WITH CANNED MALT EXTRACT

Recipes for 11 beers made with canned malt extract follow.

Basic Beer

1 56-ounce can light unhopped malt extract syrup
1 package bottom-fermenting brewer's yeast
1 package Hallertauer hop pellets (10 grams)
4 cups corn sugar
5 gallons water
1 cup corn sugar added prior to bottling

Bring 1 gallon of water to a boil in a large pot, then remove from the heat. Stir in canned malt extract and 4 cups of sugar until completely dissolved. Do not try to dissolve sugar and extract while the pot is on the stove, they will burn. After ingredients are dissolved, put the pot back on the burner and add the package of hop pellets. Bring the liquid to boil again. Boil for 10 minutes, stirring occasionally. When the mixture first comes to a boil, it tends to foam up. Watch for this and reduce heat accordingly. This will only happen once.

Pour the hot liquid into the primary fermenter and add enough cold water to produce 5 gallons. Check the temperature of the wort and add one package of brewer's yeast when the temperature is around 70 degrees Fahrenheit. Stir yeast into the wort. Cover the primary fermenter with plastic and tape and allow the mixture to ferment for two days until foam subsides. Also, cover the fermenter with a towel to exclude light.

When the foam has subsided, transfer the contents of the primary fermenter to the secondary fermenter with a siphon hose. Siphon carefully and leave the sediment behind. Fit the secondary fermenter with an air lock to exclude the atmosphere. Allow the mixture to ferment for at least five days. At first, activity—as seen by bubbles in the air lock—will be vigorous. The bubbles will slow to one or less per minute after a few days. Fermentation should be complete after five days, and specific gravity will be about 1.004 or lower. This is the time to bottle the beer.

Transfer the contents of the secondary fermenter into a 5-gallon container—the original primary fermenter, for example. Prime in bulk by adding 1 to 1.25 cups of corn sugar (dissolved in 1 cup of boiling water). While siphoning, leave sediment behind. Bottle the beer and allow it to age for six weeks. Then you can drink the beer.

The basic beer recipe lends itself well to variations:
□ Substitute hopped malt extract and omit hop pellets.
□ Add an additional package of hops when boiling the wort for a stronger beer.
□ Add 1 cup uncrushed crystal malt (whole barley grains) while boiling the wort. Strain the mixture into a primary fermenter. This addition will improve the overall taste of the beer.
□ Add one package of Burton water salts to the boiling wort.
□ Instead of hop pellets, use leaf hops (1 ounce) and boil for 30 minutes.
□ Substitute amber or dark malt extract syrup.

Light American Style Beer

1 2.5-pound can light hopped malt extract syrup
3 cups corn sugar
1 teaspoon table salt
1 package bottom-fermenting brewer's yeast
1 cup corn sugar for priming prior to bottling
5 gallons water
5 grams finishing hops—Cascade or Hallertauer pellets

Bring 1 gallon of water to boil. Remove it from the heat and dissolve 3 cups corn sugar and hopped malt extract. Reheat to a boil for 30 minutes, stirring occasionally. Add finishing hops during the last ten minutes. Strain wort into the primary fermenter. Top off with cold water to make 5 gallons and stir in yeast (with wort temperature being between 70 and 80 degrees Fahrenheit). Cover the primary fermenter and wait for two days. The foam should have subsided. Transfer the contents to the secondary fermenter, leaving sediment behind. Install an air lock and wait five to seven days. Prime with 1 cup corn sugar (dissolved in 1 cup boiling water) in bulk and bottle as usual. Specific gravity should be 1.002 or lower at the time of priming and bottling. Allow the beer to age for six weeks before drinking.

Light European Style Beer

1 3.5-pound can light hopped malt syrup
1 package bottom-fermenting brewer's yeast
3 cups corn sugar
2 teaspoons Burton water salts
.5 ounce Hallertauer finishing hops
5 gallons water
1 cup corn sugar for priming beer prior to bottling

Add Burton water salts to boiling water before the other

ingredients. Boil the wort as described in the previous recipe for 30 minutes. Add finishing hops during the last 10 minutes. Strain the wort into the primary fermenter. Add enough cold water to make 5 gallons. Add yeast when the temperature of the wort is between 70 and 80 degrees Fahrenheit. Cover and allow the mixture to ferment for two days until the foam subsides. Transfer the mixture into the secondary fermenter, leaving sediment behind. Allow the contents to ferment for five to seven days until bubbling activity in the air lock is less than one bubble per two minutes. When fermentation is complete, transfer the contents of the secondary fermenter into a clean container. Bulk prime, bottle, and age for six weeks.

Dark European Style Beer

1 *3.5-pound can dark hopped malt extract syrup*
1 *package bottom-fermenting, lager type brewer's yeast*
4 *cups corn sugar*
5 *gallons water*
.5 *ounce Hallertauer finishing hops*
2 *teaspoons Burton water salts*
1 *cup corn sugar for priming prior to bottling*

Bring 1 gallon of water to boil. Remove it from heat and dissolve Burton water salts, 4 cups corn sugar, and dark hopped malt extract syrup. Bring to boil again and allow to cook for one hour. Add finishing hops during the last 10 minutes. Strain the mixture into the primary fermenter. Add water to make 5 gallons. Add yeast (when temperature of the wort is between 70 and 80 degrees Fahrenheit) and wait two days until foam subsides. Siphon into the secondary fermenter leaving sediment behind. Install an air lock. Allow the mixture to ferment for five to seven days. Transfer the contents into a clean 5-gallon container, leaving sediment behind, and prime. Bottle the beer and let it age for six weeks.

Heinekenlike Beer

1 3.5-pound can pale unhopped malt extract syrup
1 package bottom-fermenting, lager-type brewer's yeast
2 cups corn sugar
1 pound pale unhopped dry malt extract
2 packages hop pellets
2 teaspoons Burton water salts
5 gallons water
1 cup corn sugar for priming

Bring 1 gallon of water to boil and remove from heat. Dissolve Burton water salts, 2 cups corn sugar, dry malt extract, and then a can of malt extract syrup. Add one package of hops and reheat to a boil. Boil for one hour, stirring occasionally. Add the other package of hop pellets during the last 10 minutes. Strain into the primary fermenter. Add water to make five gallons. Add yeast when the temperature is between 70 and 80 degrees Fahrenheit. Cover the primary fermenter and allow the mixture to ferment for two days until the foam subsides. Transfer the contents into the secondary fermenter, install an air lock, and allow the mixture to ferment for 7 to 10 days. Transfer the contents into a clean 5-gallon container, leaving sediment behind. Bulk prime and bottle. Age for six weeks before drinking. Chill prior to drinking to 45 degrees Fahrenheit.

Amber European Style Beer

1 3.5-pound unhopped amber malt extract
1 cup uncrushed crystal malt
1 package bottom-fermenting, lager-type brewer's yeast
2 cups corn sugar
2 teaspoons Burton water salts
2 packages pellet hops
1 cup corn sugar for priming
5 gallons water

Bring 1 gallon of water to a boil, then remove from heat. Dissolve in order: Burton water salts, 2 cups corn sugar, and a can of unhopped malt extract. Add one package of hops and 1 cup uncrushed crystal malt. Bring to a boil again. Boil for one hour, stirring occasionally. Add the other package of hops during the last 10 minutes of boiling. Remove from heat and strain into the primary fermenter. Add enough water to make 5 gallons. Add yeast when the temperature of the wort is between 70 and 80 degrees Fahrenheit. Stir in yeast, cover the primary fermenter, and allow the mixture to ferment for two days until the foam subsides. Transfer the contents into the secondary fermenter with a siphon hose, leaving sediment behind. Install an air lock and allow the mixture to ferment for 7 to 10 days. Transfer the contents into a clean 5-gallon container, leaving sediment behind. Bulk prime and bottle. Store at room temperature or below for at least six weeks before drinking. Serve the beer chilled to 45 degrees Fahrenheit.

Deep Creek Mountains Reality Beer

4 cans pale hopped malt extract syrup
16 cups white cane sugar
4 packages of hop pellets or wild hops if available (2 ounces)
4 packages bottom-fermenting, lager-type brewer's yeast
20 gallons of spring water
4 cups of white cane sugar for priming prior to bottling

This recipe was given to me by Buck Douglass, an old friend who lives in the Western Desert of Utah. While the resulting brew is a bit unorthodox, it is a good beer with a tangy, cidery taste—the results of using white sugar in the brewing. This recipe makes approximately 22 gallons of beer. If you do not have the equipment for brewing such a large quantity, divide all ingredient measures by four to arrive at a recipe for 5 gallons.

Bring 4 gallons of water to a boil. Remove from heat and

dissolve cane sugar and malt extract syrup. Add hops and boil once again for one hour. Dump the mixture into the primary fermenter and add the rest of the water. Add brewer's yeast when the temperature of the wort is between 70 and 80 degrees Fahrenheit. Allow the mixture to ferment for two to three days until foam subsides. Transfer the contents into the secondary fermenter, install an air lock, and allow the mixture to ferment for five days. Transfer the contents to a clean container, bulk prime, and bottle. Drink whether aged or not.

Light Summer Beer

1 can pale unhopped malt extract syrup
4 cups corn sugar
1 ounce dried leaf hops (domestic)
1 package bottom-fermenting, lager-type brewer's yeast
5 gallons of water
1 cup corn sugar for priming prior to bottling

Bring 1 gallon of water to a boil. Remove it from heat. Dissolve sugar and malt extract syrup. Add hops and boil again for one hour, then dump the mixture into the primary fermenter and add the rest of the water. Add brewer's yeast when the temperature of the wort is between 70 and 80 degrees Fahrenheit. Allow the mixture to ferment two to three days until foam subsides. Transfer the contents into the secondary fermenter, install air lock, and allow the mixture to ferment for five days. Transfer the contents to a clean container, bulk prime, and bottle. Age for six weeks before using.

Lowenbrau Style Beer

1 3.5-pound can unhopped amber malt extract
1 cup uncrushed crystal malt
1 package bottom-fermenting, lager-type brewer's yeast

2 *cups corn sugar*
2 *teaspoons Burton water salts*
2 *packets dried leaf hops*
1 *cup corn sugar for priming*
5 *gallons water*

Boil 1 gallon of water, then remove from heat. Dissolve in order: Burton water salts, 2 cups corn sugar, and a can of unhopped malt extract. Add one package of hops and 1 cup uncrushed crystal malt. Bring to boil again. Boil for one hour, stirring occasionally. Add the remaining package of hops during the last 10 minutes of boiling. Remove the mixture from heat and strain it into the primary fermenter. Add enough water to make 5 gallons. Add yeast when the temperature of wort is between 70 and 80 degrees Fahrenheit. Stir in yeast, cover the primary fermenter, and allow the mixture to ferment for two days until the foam subsides. Transfer the contents into the secondary fermenter with a siphon hose leaving sediment behind. Install an air lock and allow the mixture to ferment for 7 to 10 days. Transfer the contents into a clean 5-gallon container, leaving sediment behind. Bulk prime and bottle. Store at room temperature or below for at least six weeks before drinking. Serve chilled to 45 degrees Fahrenheit.

Pale European Style Beer

1   *3.5-pound can light hopped malt syrup*
1   *package bottom-fermenting brewer's yeast*
1   *package Cascade hop pellets*
3   *cups corn sugar*
2   *teaspoons Burton water salts*
.5 *ounce Hallertauer finishing hops*
5   *gallons water*
1   *cup corn sugar for priming beer prior to bottling*

Add the Burton water salts to boiling water before other

ingredients. Boil wort and hop pellets as described in the previous recipe for 30 minutes. Add finishing hops during the last 10 minutes. Strain the wort into the primary fermenter. Add enough cold water to make 5 gallons. Add yeast when the temperature of the wort is between 70 and 80 degrees Fahrenheit. Cover and allow the mixture to ferment for two days until the foam subsides. Transfer the mixture into the secondary fermenter, leaving sediment behind. Allow it to ferment for five to seven days until bubbling activity in the air lock is less than one bubble per minute. When fermentation is complete, transfer the contents of the secondary fermenter into a clean container. Bulk prime, bottle, and age for six weeks before drinking.

Tuborglike Beer

1 *3.5-pound can pale unhopped malt extract syrup*
1 *package bottom-fermenting, lager-type brewer's yeast*
2 *cups corn sugar*
1 *pound pale unhopped dry malt extract*
2 *packets hop pellets*
2 *teaspoons Burton water salts*
5 *gallons water*
1 *cup corn sugar for priming*

Boil 1 gallon of water and remove from heat. Dissolve Burton water salts, 2 cups corn sugar, dry malt extract, and malt extract syrup. Add one package of hop pellets, then reheat to a boil. Boil for one hour, stirring occasionally. Add the remaining package of hop pellets during the last 10 minutes. Strain into the primary fermenter. Add water to make 5 gallons. Add yeast when the temperature is between 70 and 80 degrees Fahrenheit. Cover the primary fermenter and allow the mixture to ferment for two days until the foam subsides. Transfer the contents into the secondary fermenter, install an air lock, and allow the mixture to ferment for 7 to 10 days. Transfer the contents into a clean 5-gallon container, leaving sediment behind. Bulk prime and bottle. Age for six weeks. Chill prior to drinking.

WHOLE GRAIN BEERS

I do not recommend that you try brewing beer with whole grains until you have mastered some basic skills in brewing with canned malt extract. When you are brewing beer from whole grains (malted barley), you are making your own malt extract. Refer to Chapter 4 if you want to review the mashing process.

Light All-Grain Beer

6 pounds pale malted barley
2 packages Hallertauer pellet hops
2 teaspoons Burton water salts
5 gallons water
1 package bottom-fermenting, lager-type brewer's yeast
1 cup corn sugar for priming beer prior to bottling

Mash the pale malted barley and add 1 teaspoonful of Burton water salts in 2 gallons of water. After the wort is run off and the grain is sparged, place the liquor in a large cooking pot. Add another teaspoon of Burton water salts, one package of pellet hops, and bring to a boil. Boil for one hour. Add the remaining package of hops during the last 10 minutes. Strain the contents into the primary fermenter. Add enough cold water to make 5 gallons. Add brewer's yeast when the temperature of the wort is between 70 and 80 degrees Fahrenheit. Allow the mixture to ferment for two days at room temperature until the foam subsides. Siphon into the secondary fermenter, leaving sediment behind. Install an air lock and allow the mixture to ferment for five to seven days. Transfer the contents to a clean 5-gallon container, leaving sediment behind. Bulk prime and bottle. Allow beer to age for six weeks at 50 to 60 degrees Fahrenheit before drinking. Serve the beer chilled to 45 degrees Fahrenheit. Specific gravity at priming time should be 1.005 or below.

Canadian Molsonlike Beer

1 3.5-pound can pale unhopped malt extract syrup
2 pounds crushed pale malted barley
2 cups corn sugar
1 package bottom-fermenting, lager-type brewer's yeast
1 teaspoon Burton water salts
3 ounces Cascade hops—dried not pellet
5 gallons water
1 cup corn sugar for priming prior to bottling

Mash the pale malted barley in 2 gallons of water to which .5 teaspoonful of Burton water salts has been added. After the wort is run off and the grain is sparged, place the liquid in a cooking pot. Add .5 teaspoonful Burton water salts, 2 cups corn sugar, malt extract syrup, and 2 ounces of hops. Boil for one hour. Add the last ounce of hops for the final 10 minutes. Stir occasionally. Strain into the primary fermenter and add cool water to make 5 gallons. Add brewer's yeast when the temperature is between 70 and 80 degrees Fahrenheit and stir. Cover the primary fermenter and allow the beer to work for two or more days until foam has subsided. Transfer contents into the secondary fermenter, leaving sediment behind. Install an air lock and allow beer to ferment for 7 to 10 days. Transfer the contents to a clean 5-gallon container, leaving sediment behind. Bulk prime and bottle. Let the beer age for six weeks at 50 to 65 degrees Fahrenheit. Specific gravity at priming time should be 1.006 or lower. Serve the beer chilled to 45 degrees Fahrenheit.

Light Becklike German Style Beer

1 2.5-pound can pale unhopped malt extract syrup
2 pounds crushed pale malted barley

3 cups corn sugar (in Germany it is illegal to use sugar)
2 packages dried Hallertauer hops—not pellet
1 teaspoon Burton water salts
1 package bottom-fermenting, lager-type brewer's yeast
5 gallons water
1 cup corn sugar for priming beer prior to bottling

Mash crushed pale malt in 2 gallons of water to which .5 teaspoonful of Burton water salts has been added. After mashing and sparging, place the liquid in a cooking pot. Add the remainder of the Burton water salts (.5 teaspoonful), 3 cups corn sugar, unhopped malt extract syrup, and one package of hops. Bring to a boil and cook for 30 minutes. Add 5 package hops and continue boiling for another 20 minutes. Add remaining hops (.5 package) and boil for an additional 10 minutes. Strain the wort into the primary fermenter. Add enough cool water to make 5 gallons. Add yeast when the temperature of the wort is between 70 and 80 degrees Fahrenheit. Cover the primary fermenter and allow the mixture to ferment for two or more days until the foam subsides. Transfer the contents into the secondary fermenter, leaving sediment behind. Install an air lock and allow the beer to ferment for 7 to 10 days. Transfer the contents to a clean 5-gallon container. Bulk prime with 1 cup corn sugar that has been dissolved in 1 cup boiling water. Specific gravity at this point should be 1.004 or lower. Bottle the beer and let it age for at least six weeks. Chill before serving.

Porter

1 pound whole black malted barley
1 pound crushed pale malted barley
1 2.5-pound can dark unhopped malt extract
2 cups corn sugar
1 package bottom-fermenting, lager-type brewer's yeast
3 ounces hops—dried but not pellet
5 gallons water

1 cup corn sugar for priming beer prior to bottling
2 teaspoons Burton water salts

Heat 2 gallons of water in a large pot to 145 degrees Fahrenheit. Add Burton water salts, black malt (whole), pale malt (crushed), 2 cups corn sugar, and malt extract syrup. Simmer for 40 minutes. Add 2 ounces of hops and boil for another 40 minutes. Add the remaining 1 ounce of hops for the last 10 minutes. Strain the liquid into the primary fermenter. Add enough cool water to make 5 gallons. Add brewer's yeast when the temperature of the wort is between 70 and 80 degrees Fahrenheit and stir. Cover the primary fermenter and allow beer to work for two days until the foam subsides. Transfer the contents into the secondary fermenter, leaving sediment behind. Ferment for 7 to 10 days. Transfer the contents to a clean 5-gallon container, leaving sediment behind. Bulk prime with 1 cup corn sugar that has been dissolved in 1 cup boiling water. Bottle the beer and let it age for six weeks before drinking. Serve at room temperature—65 degrees Fahrenheit. This is a strong, full-bodied beer that is almost like a stout. Many brewers like to mix .5 part porter with .5 part light beer to create something close to the classic Black & Tan.

Dark European Style Grain Beer

2 2.5-pound cans pale unhopped malt extract syrup
.5 pound crushed crystal malt
.5 pound whole grain malt
1 package bottom-fermenting, lager-type brewer's yeast
2 ounces dried Hallertauer hops—not pellets
1 cup corn sugar for priming prior to bottling
1 teaspoon Burton water salts
5 gallons water

Bring 2 gallons of water to a boil. Remove the heat. Dissolve Burton water salts and then unhopped pale malt extract syrup. Reheat to a boil and add one-third of the hops and the crystal malt. Boil for 40 minutes. Add black malt and the remainder of the hops. Boil for an additional 15 minutes. Strain the contents into the primary fermenter and add enough cool water to make 5 gallons. Add brewer's yeast when the temperature of the wort is between 70 and 80 degrees Fahrenheit and stir it into the liquid. Cover the primary fermenter and allow the mixture to work for two days until the foam subsides. Transfer the contents into the secondary fermenter, leaving sediment behind. Fit an air lock to the secondary fermenter and allow the mixture to ferment for five to seven days. When almost all bubbling activity has ceased, transfer the contents to a clean 5-gallon container. Prime with 1 cup of corn sugar that has been dissolved in 1 cup of boiling water. Bottle the beer and let it age for at least six weeks. Specific gravity at priming time should be 1.006 or lower. Serve at room temperature.

Amber All-Grain Beer

6 pounds crushed pale malted barley
.5 pound crushed crystal malt
.5 pound whole grain crystal malt
1 teaspoon Burton water salts
1 package bottom-fermenting, lager-type brewer's yeast
3 ounces dried Cascade hops—not pellets
1 cup corn sugar for priming beer prior to bottling
5 gallons of water

Mash the pale and crystal malt in 2 gallons of water to which .5 teaspoonful of the Burton water salts has been added. Simply heat to 158 degrees Fahrenheit and keep at this temperature for one hour. Drain the mash and sparge grains with hot water. Bring the wort to boil and add 2 ounces of hops. Boil for one hour. Add the remainder of the hops (1 ounce), whole crystal malt and .5 teaspoonful of Burton water salts during the last 10 minutes. Strain the contents into the primary fermenter and add enough cool water to make 5 gallons. Add brewer's yeast when the temperature of the wort is between 70 and 80 degrees Fahrenheit and stir. Cover the primary fermenter and allow the mixture to ferment for two days or until the foam subsides. Transfer the contents of the primary fermenter to the secondary fermenter, leaving sediment behind. Fit an air lock to the secondary fermenter and allow the mixture to work for 7 to 10 days. Transfer the contents to a clean 5-gallon container and bulk prime. Specific gravity at this point should be 1.006 or lower. Bottle the beer. Store for six weeks (at a temperature between 50 and 65 degrees Fahrenheit) before drinking. Serve chilled to 45 degrees Fahrenheit.

Mild Light Grain Beer

3 pounds crushed pale barley malt
1 pound dried pale malt extract
2 cups corn sugar
1 package hop pellets (10 grams)
2 teaspoons Burton water salts
1 package bottom-fermenting, lager-type brewer's yeast
1 cup corn sugar for priming beer prior to bottling
5 gallons water

Mash the pale malt in 2 gallons of water to which has been added 1 teaspoonful of Burton water salts. Simply bring the temperature of the water up to 158 degrees Fahrenheit. Dump in the crushed pale malted barley and cook for one hour, maintaining this temperature. Drain the mash and sparge grain. Bring the liquid to boil for one hour. Add one-third of the hops initially, one-third of the hops after 30 minutes, and the remainder for the last 10 minutes. Strain the wort into the primary fermenter, which contains 2 cups of corn sugar, 1 teaspoonful Burton water salts, and dried malt extract (pale). Add enough water to make 5 gallons. Add the brewer's yeast when the temperature of the wort is between 70 and 80 degrees Fahrenheit. Stir in the yeast, then cover the primary fermenter. Allow the beer to ferment for two days or until the foam has subsided. Transfer the contents to the secondary fermenter, leaving the sediment behind. Install an air lock. Allow the mixture to work for five or seven days. Transfer the contents of the secondary fermenter into a clean 5-gallon container, leaving sediment behind. Bulk prime with 1 cup of corn sugar that has been dissolved in 1 cup of boiling water. Bottle the beer. Specific gravity at priming time will be 1.003 or lower. Store for six weeks in a cool (50 to 65 degrees Fahrenheit) dark area before drinking. Chill to 45 degrees Fahrenheit before decanting.

Pale American Beer

1 2.5 pound can light hopped malt extract syrup
4 cups corn sugar
1 package bottom-fermenting brewer's yeast
1 cup corn sugar for priming
5 gallons water
1 package hops—Cascade or Hallertauer pellets

Bring 1 gallon of water to boil. Remove from heat and dissolve 4 cups corn sugar and hopped malt extract. Reheat to a boil for 30 minutes, stirring occasionally. Add finishing hops during the last 10 minutes. Strain the wort into the primary fermenter. Add cold water to make 5 gallons and stir in yeast (with wort temperature between 70 and 80 degrees Fahrenheit). Cover the primary fermenter and allow the mixture to work for three days until the foam subsides. Transfer the contents to the secondary fermenter, leaving sediment behind. Install an air lock and allow the mixture to work for five to seven days. When all bubbling activity has ceased, siphon the liquid into a clean 5-gallon container. Bulk prime with 1 cup of corn sugar (dissolved in 1-cup boiling water). Bottle the beer. Specific gravity should be 1.002 or lower for priming and bottling. Let the beer age for six weeks before drinking.

Dark Heavy-Hopped European Beer

1 3.5-pound can hopped malt extract syrup
1 package bottom-fermenting, lager-type brewer's yeast
4 cups corn sugar
1 package hop pellets
5 gallons water
.5 ounce Cascade finishing hops
2 teaspoons Burton water salts
1 cup corn sugar for priming

Boil 1 gallon of water and remove from heat. Dissolve Burton water salts, 4 cups of corn sugar, hop pellets, and dark hopped malt extract syrup. Bring to boil again and cook for one hour. Add finishing hops during the last 10 minutes. Strain into the primary fermenter. Add water to make 5 gallons. Add yeast when the temperature of the wort is between 70 and 80 degrees Fahrenheit. Allow the mixture to work for two days until the foam subsides. Siphon into the secondary fermenter, leaving sediment behind. Install an air lock. Let the mixture ferment for five to seven days. Transfer the contents into a clean 5-gallon container, leaving sediment behind, and prime. Bottle the beer and let it age for six weeks.

Grain Extract Light-Bodied Beer

2 pounds crushed pale malted barley
1 3.5-pound can pale unhopped malt extract syrup
2 cups corn sugar
1 package bottom-fermenting, lager-type brewer's yeast
1 teaspoon Burton water salts
3 ounces dried domestic hops—not pellet
5 gallons water
1 cup corn sugar for priming

Mash the pale malted barley in 2 gallons of water to which .5

teaspoonful of Burton water salts has been added. After the wort is run off and the grain is sparged, place the liquid in a cooking pot. Add another .5 teaspoonful Burton water salts, 2 cups corn sugar, malt extract syrup, and 2 ounces of hops. Boil for one hour. Add the last ounce of hops for the final 10 minutes. Stir occasionally. Strain into the primary fermenter and add cool water to make 5 gallons. Add brewer's yeast when the temperature is between 70 and 80 degrees Fahrenheit and stir. Cover the primary fermenter and allow the beer to work for 2 or more days until the foam has subsided. Transfer the contents into the secondary fermenter, leaving sediment behind. Install an air lock. Allow the beer to ferment for 7 to 10 days. Transfer the contents to a clean 5-gallon container, leaving sediment behind. Bulk prime and bottle. Allow the beer to age for six weeks at 50 to 65 degrees Fahrenheit. Specific gravity priming time should be 1.006 or lower. Serve the beer chilled to 45 degrees Fahrenheit.

Northern European Style Beer

1 2.5-pound can pale unhopped malt extract syrup
3 pounds crushed pale malted barley
2 cups corn sugar
2 packages dried pellet-type Hallertauer hops
1 teaspoon Burton water salts
1 package bottom-fermenting, lager-type brewer's yeast
5 gallons water
1 cup corn sugar for priming beer

Mash crushed pale malt in 2 gallons of water to which .5 teaspoonful of Burton water salts has been added. After mashing and sparging, place the liquid in a cooking pot. Add the rest of the Burton water salts, 2 cups corn sugar, malt extract syrup, and one package of hops. Bring to boil and cook for 30 minutes. Add .5 package hops and continue boiling for another 20 minutes. Add the remaining hops and boil for an additional 10 minutes. Strain the wort into the primary fermenter and add enough cool water to make 5 gallons. Add yeast when the temperature of wort is between 70 and 80 degrees Fahrenheit. Cover the primary fermenter and allow the mixture to ferment for two or more days until foam subsides. Transfer the contents into the secondary fermenter, leaving sediment behind. Install an air lock and allow the beer to ferment for 7 to 10 days. Transfer the contents to a clean 5-gallon container. Bulk prime with 1 cup boiling water. Specific gravity should be 1.004 or lower at bottling time. Bottle the beer and let it age for at least six weeks. Chill before serving.

Full-Bodied Pale All-Grain Beer

5 pounds pale malted barley
2 packages Hallertauer hops
1 package bottom-fermenting, lager-type brewer's yeast
2 teaspoons Burton water salts
5 gallons water
1 cup corn sugar for priming

Mash the pale malted barley and add 1 teaspoonful of Burton water salts in 2 gallons of water. After the wort is run off and the grain is sparged, place the liquor in a large cooking pot. Add the remaining teaspoon of Burton water salts and one package of hops. Bring to a boil. Boil for one hour. Add the other package of hops during the last 10 minutes. Strain the contents into the primary fermenter and add enough cold water to make 5 gallons. Add brewer's yeast when the temperature of the wort is between 70 and 80 degrees Fahrenheit. Allow the mixture to ferment for two days at room temperature at which time the foam will subside. Siphon into the secondary fermenter, leaving sediment behind. Install an air lock and allow the beer to ferment for five to seven days. Transfer the contents to a clean 5-gallon container, leaving sediment behind. Bulk prime and bottle. Allow the beer to age for six weeks at 50 to 65 degrees Fahrenheit before drinking. Specific gravity at priming time should be 1.005 or below. Chill to 45 degrees Fahrenheit before serving.

Australian All-Grain Beer

1 pound dried pale malt extract
2 pounds crushed pale barley malt
2 cups corn sugar
1 package hop pellets
2 teaspoons Burton water salts
1 package bottom-fermenting, lager-type brewer's yeast
1 cup corn sugar for priming beer
5 gallons water

Mash the pale malt in 2 gallons of water to which 1 teaspoonful of Burton water salts has been added. Bring the temperature of the water up to 158 degrees Fahrenheit. Dump in the crushed pale malted barley and cook for one hour, maintaining this temperature. Drain the mash and sparge grain. Bring the liquid to boil for one hour. Add one-third of the hops initially, one-third of the hops after 30 minutes, and the remainder for the last 10 minutes. Strain the wort into the primary fermenter, which contains 2 cups of corn sugar, 1 teaspoonful Burton water salts, and dried malt extract (pale). Add enough water to make 5 gallons. Add the brewer's yeast when the temperature of the wort is between 70 and 80 degrees Fahrenheit. Stir in the yeast, then cover the primary fermenter. Allow the beer to ferment for two days or until the foam has subsided. Transfer the contents to the secondary fermenter, leaving the sediment behind. Install an air lock and allow the mixture to work for five to seven days. Transfer the contents of a secondary fermenter into a clean 5-gallon container, leaving the sediment behind. Bulk prime with 1 cup of corn sugar that has been dissolved in 1 cup of boiling water. Bottle the beer. Specific gravity at priming time is 1.003 or lower. Store the beer in a cool (50 degrees Fahrenheit) dark area for six weeks before drinking. Chill to 45 degrees Fahrenheit before serving.

Dark Pilsner Number One

1 pound whole black malted barley
1 pound crushed pale malted barley
1 2.5-pound can dark unhopped malt extract
2 cups corn sugar
2 teaspoons Burton water salts
1 package bottom-fermenting, lager-type brewer's yeast
3 ounces pellet-type hops
5 gallons water
1 cup corn sugar for priming beer

Heat 2 gallons of water in a large pot to 145 degrees Fahrenheit. Add Burton water salts, black malt (whole), pale malt (crushed), 2 cups corn sugar, and malt extract syrup. Simmer for 40 minutes. Add 2 ounces of hops and boil for another 40 minutes. Add the remaining 1 ounce of hops for the last 10 minutes. Strain the liquid into the primary fermenter and add enough cool water to make 5 gallons. Add brewer's yeast when the temperature of the wort is between 70 and 80 degrees Fahrenheit and stir. Cover the primary fermenter and allow beer to work for two days until the foam subsides. Transfer the contents into the secondary fermenter, leaving sediment behind. Ferment for 7 to 10 days. Transfer the contents to a clean 5-gallon container, leaving sediment behind. Bulk prime with 1 cup corn sugar that has been dissolved in 1 cup boiling water. Bottle the beer and let it age for six weeks before drinking. Serve at room temperature—65 degrees Fahrenheit. This is a strong, full-bodied beer.

Dark Pilsner Number Two

2 2.5-pound cans pale unhopped malt extract syrup

1 pound crushed crystal malt
.5 pound whole grain black malt
1 package bottom-fermenting, lager-type brewer's yeast
2 ounces hop pellets
1 cup corn sugar for priming beer
1 teaspoon Burton water salts
5 gallons water

Bring 2 gallons of water to a rapid boil. Remove from heat and dissolve Burton water salts and pale malt extract syrup. Reheat to a boil and add one-half of the hops and the crystal malt. Boil for 40 minutes. Add black malt and the rest of the hops. Boil for an additional 15 minutes. Strain contents into the primary fermenter and add enough cool water to make 5 gallons. Add brewer's yeast when the temperature of the wort is between 70 and 80 degrees Fahrenheit and stir it into the liquid. Cover the primary fermenter and allow the mixture to work for two days until the foam subsides. Transfer the contents into the secondary fermenter, leaving sediment behind. Install an air lock and allow the beer to ferment for five to seven days. When almost all bubbling has ceased, transfer the contents to a clean 5-gallon container. Prime with 1 cup of corn sugar that has been dissolved in 1 cup of boiling water. Bottle the beer and let it age for at least six weeks. Specific gravity at priming time should be 1.006 or lower. Serve at room temperature.

Golden Grain Beer

4 pounds crushed pale malted barley
1 pound crushed crystal malt
1 pound crystal malt—whole grains
1 teaspoon Burton water salts
1 package bottom-fermenting, lager-type brewer's yeast
3 ounces dried Saaz hop clusters
1 cup corn sugar for priming beer
5 gallons water

Mash the crushed pale and crystal malt in 2 gallons of water to which .5 teaspoonful of Burton water salts has been added. Heat to 158 degrees Fahrenheit and keep mashing at this temperature for one hour. Drain the mash and sparge grains with hot water. Bring the wort to boil and add 2 ounces of hops. Boil for one hour. Add the rest of the hops (1 ounce), the whole crystal malt, and .5 teaspoonful of Burton water salts during the last 10 minutes. Strain the contents into the primary fermenter and add enough cool water to make 5 gallons. Add brewer's yeast when the temperature of the wort is between 70 and 80 degrees Fahrenheit and stir. Cover the primary fermenter and allow the beer to ferment for two days or until the foam subsides. Transfer the contents to the secondary fermenter, leaving sediment behind. Fit an air lock to the secondary fermenter and allow the beer to work for 8 to 10 days. Transfer the contents to a clean 5-gallon container and bulk prime. Specific gravity at bottling time should be 1.006 or lower. Bottle the beer and store it for six weeks (at a temperature between 50 and 65 degrees Fahrenheit) before drinking. Serve the beer chilled to 45 degrees Fahrenheit.

ALES

Brewing with top-fermenting yeasts results in brews that are ales or stouts. Ales generally are much more robust than lagers. They also tend to be darker and have a sharper, more pronounced hop flavor. It takes time to develop a fondness for ale. Most ales also have a higher alcoholic content than lagers. All the standard brewing techniques discussed so far also apply to brewing ales. The only main differences are the yeast used and additional amounts of ingredients. You really owe it to yourself (and your drinking friends) to brew up a batch of ale every so often. I brew ales about once every three batches of beer.

Pale Ale

2 pounds crushed pale malted barley

.5 pound crushed crystal malt
.5 pound crystal malt—whole grains
1 3.5-pound can pale unhopped malt extract syrup
3 ounces Fuggles dried hops—not pellets
6 teaspoons Burton water salts
1 package bottom-fermenting yeast for ale
1 cup corn sugar for priming just prior to bottling
5 gallons water

Mash crushed pale and crystal malted barley grain in 2 gallons of water to which 1 teaspoonful of Burton water salts has been added. Bring the temperature of the water up to 158 degrees Fahrenheit. Add the crushed grain (and salts) and maintain this temperature for one hour. Drain the mash and sparge the grain to recover more extract. Place the liquid in a large cooking pot and bring to a boil. Add 2.5 ounces of the Fuggles hops and boil for 45 minutes. Add the last .5 ounce of hops, the rest of the Burton water salts, and uncrushed crystal malt. Boil for another 10 minutes. Strain the wort into the primary fermenter. Add unhopped malt extract syrup and enough cool water to make 5 gallons. Make certain that the extract syrup is dissolved before adding cool water. When the temperature of the wort is between 70 and 80 degrees Fahrenheit, add the top-fermenting yeast for ale and stir. Allow the wort to ferment for two or more days until the foam subsides. Transfer the contents into the secondary fermenter, leaving the sediment behind. Fit an air lock to the secondary fermenter and allow the ale to ferment for five to seven days. When specific gravity is 1.008 or below transfer the contents of the secondary fermenter into a clean 5-gallon container. Bulk prime with 1 cup of sugar that has been dissolved in 1 cup of boiling water. Bottle the ale. Store it undisturbed for six weeks between 50 and 65 degrees Fahrenheit. Serve the ale chilled to 45 degrees Fahrenheit after decanting.

Amber Ale Made from Extract

1 3.5-pound can amber hopped malt extract syrup

4 cups (approximately 2 pounds) pale dried malt extract
6 teaspoons Burton water salts
1 ounce Fuggles flavoring hops
.5 ounce finishing hops
1 package top-fermenting brewer's yeast for ale
5 gallons water
1 cup corn sugar for priming ale prior to bottling

Bring 2 gallons of water to boil, then remove from the heat. Dissolve Burton water salts. Add canned amber malt extract, dried malt extract, and 1 ounce of flavoring hops. Boil for 40 minutes, then add finishing hops and boil for an additional 10 minutes. Strain into the primary fermenter and add enough water to make 5 gallons. When the temperature of the wort is between 70 and 80 degrees Fahrenheit, stir in the ale yeast. Cover the primary fermenter. Let the ale work for two days or until the foam subsides. Transfer the contents of the primary fermenter to the secondary fermenter, leaving the sediment behind. Fit with an air lock. Allow the ale to ferment for five to seven days. The specific gravity will be 1.007 or below. Transfer the contents to a clean 5-gallon container. Bulk prime with 1 cup of corn sugar dissolved in 1 cup of boiling water. Bottle the ale. Age at temperatures ranging from 50 to 65 degrees Fahrenheit for six weeks. Chill the ale before serving.

Red Devil Ale

1 3.5-pound can pale hopped malt extract syrup
1 pound crystal malt—whole grain
4 teaspoons Burton water salts
1 ounce Brewer's Gold flavoring hops
.5 ounce Cascade finishing hops
1 package top-fermenting brewer's yeast for ale
5 gallons water
1 cup corn sugar for priming prior to bottling

Bring 2 gallons of water to a boil, then remove from the heat.

Dissolve 4 teaspoons of Burton water salts. Stir in canned pale hopped malt extract syrup, 1 pound of crystal malt, and flavoring hops. Bring the wort to boil for one hour. Add finishing hops for the last 10 minutes. Strain into the primary fermenter and add enough water to make 5 gallons. When the temperature of the wort is between 70 and 80 degrees Fahrenheit, add the top-fermenting ale yeast and stir. Cover the primary fermenter and allow the ale to work for at least two days until the foam subsides. Transfer the contents into the secondary fermenter and fit with an air lock. Allow the ale to ferment for 7 to 10 days. The specific gravity will be at or below 1.007. Transfer the contents to a clean 5-gallon container. Bulk prime with 1 cup of corn sugar that has been dissolved in 1 cup of boiling water. Bottle the ale. Let it age (at from 50 to 65 degrees Fahrenheit for six weeks. Chill to 45 degrees Fahrenheit and decant before serving.

Strong Ale

7 pounds crushed pale malted barley
1 pound crushed crystal malt
.5 pound flaked corn
.5 pound flaked wheat
4 ounces hops
1 pound dried pale malt extract
1 package top-fermenting brewer's yeast for ale
1 cup corn sugar for priming ale prior to bottling
5 gallons water
6 teaspoonsful Burton water salts

Cook the adjuncts (corn and wheat) in water until they are a gelatinous mass. Add the adjuncts to the mash. Cook at 158 degrees Fahrenheit for one hour. Drain mash, sparge grains, and put the liquid into a cooking pot. Add dried malt extract and 2 ounces of hops. Bring to a boil and add 1 ounce of hops after 30 minutes. Continue boiling for another 30 minutes. Add the remainder of the hops (1 ounce) for the last 10 minutes. Strain the wort into the primary fermenter. Add enough cool water to make 5 gallons. When the temperature of the wort is between 70 and 80 degrees Fahrenheit, add top-fermenting, ale-type yeast. Stir the yeast into the wort and cover the primary fermenter. Allow the ale to work for at least two days or until the foam subsides. Transfer the contents to a clean secondary fermenter and fit with an air lock. Let the ale ferment for 7 to 10 days. The specific gravity will then be 1.010 or lower. Transfer the contents to a clean 5-gallon container. Bulk prime with 1 cup of corn sugar that has been dissolved in 1 cup of boiling water. Bottle the ale and store it at between 50 and 65 degrees Fahrenheit for six weeks. Chill and decant before serving.

Tiger Ale

5 pounds crushed pale malt
.5 pound crushed crystal malt
2 cups corn sugar
2 ounces Fuggles hops—not pellets
1 package top-fermenting yeast for ale
5 gallons water
2 teaspoons Burton water salts
1 cup corn sugar for priming

Mash the crushed malt in water to which the Burton water salts have been added. Drain the mash, sparge grains, and put the liquid into the cooking pot. Add 2 cups of corn sugar and stir. Add 1 ounce of hops. Place the mixture on the stove to boil for 30 minutes. Add remaining hops (1 ounce) for the last 10 minutes of boiling. Pour the contents into the primary fermenter. Add enough cool water to make 5 gallons. Add top-fermenting, ale-type yeast when the temperature of the liquid is between 70 and 80 degrees Fahrenheit. Cover the primary fermenter and allow the ale to work for two to three days or until the foam subsides. Siphon the liquid into the secondary fermenter, leaving the sediment behind. Fit with an air lock and allow the ale to ferment for 7 to 10 days. When all activity stops, siphon the ale into a clean container. Bulk prime with 1 cup of sugar that has been dissolved in 1 cup of boiling water. Bottle the ale and store it in a cool (50 degrees Fahrenheit) dark area for six weeks. Serve at room temperature.

Draft Horse Ale

6 pounds crushed pale malted barley
1 pound crushed crystal malt
1 pound flaked corn
4 ounces hops
1 pound dried pale malt extract
1 package top-fermenting brewer's yeast for ale
1 cup corn sugar for priming ale prior to bottling
5 gallons water
6 teaspoonsful Burton water salts

Cook the flaked corn in water until it becomes a gelatinous mass. Add it to the mash. Cook at 158 degrees Fahrenheit for one hour. Drain the mash, sparge grains, and put the liquid into a cooking pot. Add dried malt extract and 2 ounces of hops. Bring to a boil. Add 1 ounce of hops after 30 minutes. Continue boiling for another 30 minutes. Add the remainder of the hops for the last 10 minutes. Strain the wort into the primary fermenter and add enough cool water to make 5 gallons. When the temperature of the wort is between 70 and 80 degrees Fahrenheit, add top-fermenting ale-type yeast. Stir the yeast into the wort and cover the primary fermenter. Let the ale work for at least two days or until the foam subsides. Transfer the contents to a clean secondary fermenter and install an air lock. Let the ale ferment for 7 to 10 days. The specific gravity then will be 1.010 or lower. Transfer the contents to a clean 5-gallon container. Bulk prime with 1 cup of corn sugar that has been dissolved in 1 cup of boiling water. Bottle the ale and store it at between 50 and 65 degrees Fahrenheit for six weeks. Chill and decant before serving. This ale tastes strong and is not recommended for the inexperienced beer drinker.

Australian Sundowner's Ale

1 3.5-pound can pale hopped malt extract syrup
1.5 pounds crystal malt—whole grain
4 teaspoons Burton water salts
1 ounce imported flavoring hops
.5 ounce Cascade finishing hops
1 package top-fermenting brewer's yeast for ale
5 gallons water
1 cup corn sugar for priming prior to bottling

Bring 2 gallons of water to a boil, then remove it from the heat. Dissolve Burton water salts. Stir in canned malt extract syrup, crystal malt, and flavoring hops. Bring the wort to a boil for one hour. Add finishing hops for the last 10 minutes. Strain into the primary fermenter and add enough water to make 5 gallons. When the temperature of the wort is between 70 and 80 degrees Fahrenheit, add the top-fermenting yeast and stir. Cover the primary fermenter. Let the ale work for at least two days until the foam subsides. Transfer the contents into the secondary fermenter and attach an air lock. Let the ale ferment for 7 to 10 days. The specific gravity then will be at or below 1.007. Transfer the contents to a clean 5-gallon container. Bulk prime with 1 cup of corn sugar that has been dissolved in 1 cup of boiling water. Bottle the ale and let it age (from 50 to 65 degrees Fahrenheit) for six weeks. Chill to 45 degrees Fahrenheit before serving.

Golden Ale

1 3.5-pound can amber hopped malt extract syrup
2 pounds pale dried malt extract

6 teaspoons Burton water salts
1 ounce Saaz flavoring hops
.5 ounce finishing hops
1 package top-fermenting brewer's yeast for ale
5 gallons water
1 cup corn sugar for priming ale prior to bottling

Bring 2 gallons of water to a boil, then remove from the heat. Dissolve Burton water salts. Add canned malt extract, dried malt extract, and 1 ounce of flavoring hops. Boil for 40 minutes, then add finishing hops and boil for another 10 minutes. Strain into the primary fermenter and add enough water to make 5 gallons. When the temperature of the wort is between 70 and 80 degrees Fahrenheit, stir in the yeast. Cover the primary fermenter. Let the ale work for two days or until the foam subsides. Transfer the contents of the primary fermenter to the secondary fermenter, leaving the sediment behind. Fit with an air lock and allow the ale to ferment for five to seven days. The specific gravity then will be 1.007 or below. Transfer the contents to a clean 5-gallon container. Bulk prime with 1 cup of corn sugar dissolved in 1 cup of boiling water. Bottle the ale. Age it at temperatures ranging from 50 to 65 degrees Fahrenheit for six weeks. Chill to 45 degrees Fahrenheit before serving.

Murphy's Ale

3 pounds crushed pale malted barley
1 pound crushed crystal malt
1 pound crystal malt—whole grains
1 3.5-pound can pale unhopped malt extract syrup
3 ounces domestic dried hops, not pellets
6 teaspoons Burton water salts
1 package bottom-fermenting yeast for ale
1 cup corn sugar for priming prior to bottling
5 gallons water

Mash the crushed pale and crystal malted barley grain in 2

gallons of water to which 1 teaspoonful of Burton water salts has been added. To simplify the mashing, bring the temperature of the water up to 158 degrees Fahrenheit. Add the crushed grain and salts. Maintain this temperature for one hour. Drain the mash and sparge the grain to recover more extract. Place the liquid in a large cooking pot and bring to a boil. Add 2 ounces of the hops and boil for 45 minutes. Add the last ounce of hops, the rest of the Burton water salts, and the uncrushed crystal malt. Boil for 10 more minutes. Strain the wort into the primary fermenter. Add unhopped malt extract syrup and enough cool water to make 5 gallons. Make certain that the extract syrup is dissolved before adding cool water. When the temperature of the wort is between 70 and 80 degrees Fahrenheit, add the top-fermenting yeast and stir. Let the wort ferment for two or more days until the foam subsides. Transfer the contents into the secondary fermenter, leaving the sediment behind. Fit an air lock to the secondary fermenter. Allow the ale to ferment for five to seven days. When the specific gravity is 1.008 or below, transfer the contents of the secondary fermenter into a clean 5-gallon container. Bulk prime with 1 cup of sugar that has been dissolved in 1 cup of boiling water. Bottle the ale and store it undisturbed for six weeks at between 50 and 65 degrees Fahrenheit in a dark area. Serve the ale chilled to 45 degrees Fahrenheit.

STOUTS

Stouts are also brewed with top-fermenting yeasts. Stouts are always dark in color and full of flavor. Because of the strength of stout, many people do not like the taste. It is difficult to find stout in the United States. While the taste of a good stout tends to be a bit overpowering, an excellent beverage can be made by mixing equal amounts of stout and a light or pale beer.

Lightweight Stout

2 3.5-pound cans dark hopped malt extract syrup

.5 ounce Cascade hops—dried and compressed
1 package top-fermenting brewer's yeast for ale
1 cup corn sugar for priming the stout before bottling
5 gallons water

Bring 2 gallons of water to a boil. Remove from the heat and stir in the dark hopped malt extract syrup until dissolved. Boil the wort for one hour. Add finishing hops for the last 10 minutes. Strain into the primary fermenter and add enough cool water to make 5 gallons. When the temperature of the wort is between 70 and 80 degrees Fahrenheit, stir in the top-fermenting yeast. Cover the primary fermenter and allow the stout to work for three to four days until foam subsides. Transfer the contents to a clean secondary fermenter and install an air lock. Allow the stout to ferment until all activity has ceased—generally longer than beer or ale and possibly as long as 10 to 12 days. The high concentration of malt makes fermentation take longer. When specific gravity is 1.015 or below, transfer the contents of the secondary fermenter into a clean 5-gallon container. Bulk prime with 1 cup of corn sugar that has been dissolved in 1 cup of boiling water. Small 8-ounce bottles are best for bottling the stout. Let the stout age for at least three months before drinking. Serve at room temperature.

Dublin Stout

2 3.5-pound cans dark unhopped malt extract syrup
1 pound crushed crystal malt
.5 pound crushed black malt
4 teaspoons Burton water salts
4 ounces Fuggles hops
1 package top-fermenting brewer's yeast for ale
1 cup corn sugar for priming prior to bottling
5 gallons water

Bring two gallons of water to a rapid boil, then remove from heat. Dissolve Burton water salts, then two cans of dark malt extract syrup. Reheat to a boil. Add crystal and black malt and 3 ounces of hops. Boil for one hour. Add the rest of the hops (1 ounce) during the last five minutes. Strain into the primary fermenter and add enough cool water to make 5 gallons. When the temperature of the wort is between 70 and 80 degrees Fahrenheit stir in the top-fermenting yeast. Cover the primary fermenter and allow the stout to work for at least three days until the foam subsides. Transfer the contents into a clean secondary fermenter, leaving sediment behind. Fit with an air lock and allow the stout to ferment for at least 10 days. Specific gravity will be around 1.015 after fermentation is complete. Transfer the contents into a clean 5-gallon container. Bulk prime with 1 cup of corn sugar that has been dissolved in 1 cup of boiling water. Eight-ounce bottles are best for bottling. Age for at least three months before serving at room temperature.

Real Man's Stout

2 3.5-pound cans dark unhopped malt extract syrup
.5 pound lightly crushed black malt
2 pounds crushed pale malt
2 ounces Hallertauer hops—pellet form
1 package top-fermenting brewer's yeast for ale
4 teaspoons Burton water salts
.125 ounce licorice
1 cup corn sugar for priming prior to bottling
5 gallons water

Bring 2 gallons of water to a boil, then remove from the heat. Dissolve Burton water salts. Stir in malt extract syrup. Bring the wort to a boil. Add lightly crushed grains and 1.5 ounces of hops. Boil for one hour. Add the rest of the hops (.5 ounce) during the last 10 minutes. Strain into the primary fermenter and add enough water to make 5 gallons. Add licorice at this time. When the temperature of the wort is between 70 and 80 degrees Fahrenheit, stir in the top-fermenting yeast. Cover and allow the stout to ferment for at least three days or until the foam subsides. Transfer the contents into a clean secondary fermenter, leaving sediment behind. Fit with an air lock and let the stout ferment for at least 10 days. The specific gravity then will be 1.030 or higher. When the hydrometer reading remains constant for two days, it's time to bottle. Transfer the contents of the secondary fermenter into a clean 5-gallon container. Bulk prime with 1 cup of corn sugar that has been dissolved in 1 cup of boiling water. Bottles of 8 or less ounces are best. Store and age the stout from 50 to 65 degrees Fahrenheit for at least three months. Serve at room temperature.

Buccaneer Stout

2 3.5-pound cans dark unhopped malt extract syrup
1 pound lightly crushed black malt
2 pounds crushed pale malt
2 ounces imported hops—pellet form
1 package top-fermenting brewer's yeast for ale
4 teaspoons Burton water salts
1 cup corn sugar for priming prior to bottling
5 gallons water

Bring 2 gallons of water to a boil, then remove from the heat. Dissolve Burton water salts. Stir in malt extract syrup. Bring the wort to a boil again. Add crushed grains and 1.5 ounces of hops. Boil for one hour. Add the rest of the hops (.5 ounce) during the last 10 minutes. Strain into the primary fermenter and add enough water to make 5 gallons. When the temperature of the wort is between 70 and 80 degrees Fahrenheit, stir in the top-fermenting yeast. Cover the stout and let it ferment for at least three days or until the foam subsides. Transfer the contents into a clean secondary fermenter, leaving sediment behind. Fit with an air lock. Let the stout ferment for at least 10 days. The specific gravity then will be 1.030 or higher. When the reading on the hydrometer remains constant for two days, it is time to bottle. Transfer the contents of the secondary fermenter into a clean 5-gallon container. Bulk prime with 1 cup of corn sugar that has been dissolved in 1 cup of boiling water. Bottle the stout in small bottles. Store and age the stout from 50 to 65 degrees Fahrenheit for at least three months. Serve at room temperature.

Shamrock Stout

2 3.5-pound cans dark unhopped malt extract syrup
2 pounds crushed crystal malt
1 pound crushed black malt
4 teaspoons Burton water salts
4 ounces Saaz hops
1 package top-fermenting brewer's yeast for ale
1 cup corn sugar for priming prior to bottling
5 gallons water

Bring 2 gallons of water to boil, then remove from the heat. Dissolve Burton water salts, then dark malt extract syrup. Reheat to a boil. Add crystal and black malt and 3 ounces of hops. Boil for one hour. Add the rest of the hops (1 ounce) during the last 10 minutes. Strain into the primary fermenter and add enough cool water to make 5 gallons. When the temperature of the work is between 70 and 80 degrees Fahrenheit, stir in the top-fermenting yeast. Cover the primary fermenter. Allow the stout to work for at least three days until the foam subsides. Transfer the contents into a clean secondary fermenter, leaving the sediment behind. Fit with an air lock. Let the stout ferment for at least 10 days. Specific gravity will be around 1.015 after fermentation is complete. Transfer the contents into a clean 5-gallon container. Bulk prime with 1 cup of corn sugar that has been dissolved in 1 cup of boiling water. Bottle the stout; again, small bottles are best. Age for at least three months before serving at room temperature.

Mild Stout

2 3.5-pound cans dark hopped malt extract syrup

1 ounce imported dried leaf hops
1 package top-fermenting brewer's yeast for ale
1 cup corn sugar for priming the stout before bottling
5 gallons water

Bring 2 gallons of water to a boil. Remove from the heat and stir in the malt extract syrup until dissolved. Boil the wort for one hour. Add hops for the last 10 minutes. Strain into the primary fermenter and add enough cool water to make 5 gallons. When the temperature of the wort is between 70 and 80 degrees Fahrenheit, stir in the top-fermenting yeast. Cover the primary fermenter and allow the stout to work for four to six days until the foam subsides. Transfer the contents to a clean secondary fermenter and install an air lock. Allow the stout to ferment until all activity has stopped—possibly as long as 10 to 12 days. The high concentration of malt makes fermentation take longer. When specific gravity is 1.015 or below, transfer the contents of the secondary fermenter into a clean 5-gallon container. Bulk prime with 1 cup of corn sugar that has been dissolved in 1 cup of boiling water. Bottle the stout and let it age for at least three months before drinking. Serve at room temperature. If the taste proves too strong, mix equal amounts of beer and stout for a milder drink.

Medicinal Stout

1 pound black malt—whole grains
1 pound crystal malt—whole grains
1 ounce dried hop leaf
.5 ounce licorice root
2 large potatoes
2 ounces brown sugar
1 package top-fermenting yeast for ale
1 gallon water

Bring the gallon of water to a boil. Remove it from the heat while you add the following: black malt, crystal malt, hops, licorice root, and two large potatoes (these should be washed and pricked all over with a fork—leave skins on). Boil for one hour. Remove from heat. Strain into the fermenter, then stir in brown sugar to dissolve. When the temperature is between 70 and 80 degrees Fahrenheit, stir in the yeast. Cover and let the stout work for two days. Siphon the contents into a clean secondary fermenter, leaving sediment behind. Fit with an air lock. Let the stout ferment for one week or until all activity stops. Siphon the liquid into a clean container and then bottle. Do not prime with sugar. This stout, which is said to calm the system, is ready to drink after six weeks. It can be stored for up to two years.

Alcoholic Beverages

The recipes in this chapter include several types of *liqueurs* and *cordials*. Vodka is used as a base liquid in these recipes. This is done so that you can produce a quality liqueur or cordial in a minimum amount of time. While you can make these drinks using basic ingredients and some specialized equipment this is really an area that cannot possibly be covered here. There are also strict federal and state regulations regarding the making of beverages with a high alcoholic content. To my knowledge, no regulations exist when vodka is used as a base.

The two basic types of vodka available are 80 and 100 proof. If vodka is listed in a recipe, you may use the lower proof vodka. When purchasing vodka for these recipes, buy the cheapest you can find. You need be concerned only with the alcoholic content of the vodka—not the taste. Another good reason for choosing the cheapest vodka, and vodka martini drinkers might argue with me on this point, is that all vodka tastes the same. Why spend more than you have to for a vodka that will only be used as a base for a liqueur?

All the recipes given in this chapter require fresh fruits for flavoring. If you obtain your fruit from a supermarket or farm stand, chances are very good that the fruit was commercially produced and therefore sprayed with an insecticide. Wash the fruit prior to use. Carefully look over the fruit and remove any dirt or other foreign material. You want to extract the fruit essence and no other flavors.

In some cases a liqueur or cordial must be filtered before bottling. The easiest way to do this is to use a large funnel lined with cheesecloth. When working with vodka, remember that this liquid evaporates quickly. If the filtering takes a long time, cover the top of the funnel with plastic wrap after filling to prevent excess evaporation of the alcohol.

Homemade liqueurs and cordials store very well as a result of their alcoholic content. When storing, make sure that the container is sealed tightly, or the alcohol will evaporate. Alcohol is a much better preservative than salt, vinegar, or sugar. Alcohol often enhances the taste and flavor of other ingredients. An orange has more flavor after it has been *pickled* in vodka for several months.

APRICOT LIQUEUR

1 pound freshly picked apricots
1.5 cups white sugar
1 quart vodka (higher proof)

Prick the skins of the apricots all over with a pointed kitchen tool such as a cake tester or toothpick. Place them in a gallon glass jar, add the sugar, and pour in the vodka. Swirl the mixture to dissolve the sugar and allow it to sit for 24 hours. Remove the fruit and bottle the liqueur. Strain through filter paper or cheesecloth to remove bits of apricots, if necessary.

Store for a minimum of three months at room temperature before drinking.

An alternate recipe that produces a deeper apricot flavor uses the following ingredients:

2 cups apricot pits
1.5 cups sugar
1 quart vodka (higher proof)

Place the pits, sugar, and vodka in a gallon glass jar. Swirl to dissolve the sugar and cover. Allow the liqueur to sit for one month; stir daily. Strain and filter if necessary, then bottle. Store at room temperature for another two months. The liqueur is then ready to drink.

BLUEBERRY LIQUEUR

2 pounds fresh picked blueberries
.5 cup sugar
1 quart vodka

Carefully look over the blueberries and discard any that are damaged. It is not necessary to wash the blueberries unless they have been sprayed or are soiled. Gently crush the blueberries and place them—stems and all—in a gallon glass jar. Add the sugar and vodka and swirl to dissolve the sugar. Cover tightly and let the mixture sit for one month. Agitate the container daily. The container should be placed in a dark area at room temperature. Label the container with the starting date and the date that the liqueur will be ready. After one month, filter and strain the liqueur and bottle. Let it sit in storage for another two months before drinking.

This recipe produces a light-colored blueberry liqueur. If you want a liqueur with a darker color, decrease the amount of blueberries by about 2 tablespoons and substitute an equal amount of blackberries. The blackberries will give the liqueur a deep purple color, but they will not affect the rich blueberry flavor.

CHERRY LIQUEUR

1 pound fresh picked black cherries
.5 cup sugar
2 cups vodka
2 cups kirsch or curacao

Carefully inspect the cherries and remove any damaged fruit, stems, and any foreign material. Wash the fruit and let it dry. Crush all the cherries with a potato masher to expose the pits. Place the crushed fruit in a clean glass gallon jug and cover. Let it sit for 24 hours and then add the sugar, vodka, and other liqueur. Cover tightly and swirl to dissolve the sugar. Let the mixture sit for about one month in a dark area at room temperature. Agitate it daily. Strain, filter, and bottle after one month. Store for at least two more months before drinking.

An alternate method of making cherry liqueur is to use 2 cups of cherry pits rather than crushed fruit. Place the pits and all other ingredients in a clean glass gallon jar. Cover the ingredients tightly and let them age for one month with daily agitation. Strain, filter, and bottle after one month. Let the clear liqueur age for another two months before drinking.

CHAMOMILE LIQUEUR

4 tablespoons chamomile flowers
2 cups vodka
2 cups dry white wine

1 cup sugar
.5 cup honey

This cordial will appeal to you if you are fond of the mild flavor of chamomile. Many people feel that freshly picked chamomile will produce a drink with a better flavor than if dried flowers are used. If dried flowers are used, cut the amount given above (fresh flowers) in half.

Place all the ingredients in a clean glass gallon jar. Cover tightly and shake to dissolve and mix. Let the mixture stand for one week with daily agitation. Most of the flowers will have sunk to the bottom of the jar. Strain and filter the liqueur and bottle it. Let it age for two months before drinking.

COFFEE LIQUEUR

.25 cup instant coffee crystals
1 vanilla bean pod
2 cups sugar
2 cups boiling water
1 quart vodka

This recipe makes a drink that is almost identical to the popular Kahlua brand of coffee-flavored liqueur. A decaffeinated version can be made by substituting decaffeinated instant coffee.

Boil the water and mix in the instant coffee. When the liquid cools, dump it into a clean glass container and add the sugar, vodka, and vanilla bean. Stir to dissolve the sugar. Cover and let it sit for one month with daily agitation. Remove the vanilla bean (which can be used many times) and bottle the liqueur. Let it age in a dark area, at room temperature, for two months before drinking.

An alternate method of making this coffee-flavored liqueur is to use 1 pint of dark Karo syrup instead of white sugar. This will result in a heavier liquid that is almost like a syrup, but it tastes great.

GIN

.5 cup fresh juniper berries or .25 cup of dried berries
1 quart vodka—100 proof
1 cup sugar
.5 cup boiling water

You can make a very flavorful gin that is excellent in martinis. The alcoholic content is also higher than that of standard gins on the market. If you live in the western part of the country where juniper trees dominate, as they do in my home state of Utah, the berries from this tree can be had for the picking. The best time to pick juniper berries is in September and October.

Place .5 cup of fresh juniper berries (or .25 cup of dried berries) in a clean gallon glass jar. Pour in 1 quart of 100 proof vodka. Seal tightly and store for one month. Shake the container every other day. Add 1 cup of sugar (that has been dissolved in .5 cup of boiling water) to the gin. The sugar syrup should be cool *before adding*. Strain the sugar/gin mixture and bottle. Let the filtered gin age for at least six months before drinking. This gin is best when served very cold with a twist of lemon peel.

HONEY CORDIAL

2 cups vodka
3 tablespoons ground orange peel
1 pound honey
1 cup water
1 clove
1 cinnamon stick (optional)

This recipe produces an orange-flavored cordial that is very smooth tasting and also excellent in many dessert recipes. Mix the orange peel and vodka in a clean glass jar and cover tightly. Let it sit for two weeks. Agitate daily. Boil the water and stir in the honey to dissolve. When this sugary liquid cools, add it to the vodka/orange peel liquid. Let this mixture stand, with occasional agitation, for two weeks. Strain and filter the cordial. Bottle and let it age for another two months before drinking.

ORANGE LIQUEUR

8 fresh oranges
4 fresh lemons
1 quart vodka (strong—100 proof)
2 cups water
2 pounds sugar

This recipe produces a standard orange base liqueur that is very similar to the French Grand Marnier. It is simple to make and is an excellent substitute in dessert recipes requiring an orange base liqueur.

Peel the oranges and lemons, taking as little of the white underside of the skin as possible. Cut the peels into thin strips and place in a clean gallon glass container, then add the vodka. Boil the water and dissolve the sugar. When this cools, add it to the orange and lemon rinds liquid. Cover tightly and shake well. Let this liquid sit for two weeks. Shake the container every other day or so. Strain and filter the liquid after two weeks then bottle. Let the orange liqueur age for at least six weeks before using.

PEACH LIQUEUR

3 cups peach pits

1 quart vodka (higher proof)
3 cups sugar
3 cups water

I have been making this classic liqueur for almost a decade. It is a wonderfully pleasant drink that also makes an excellent gift for the holidays.

Scrub the exterior of each peach pit with a stiff bristled brush to remove as much of the peach particles as possible. You want to use only the pits and almost none of the peach fruit. Place the cleaned pits in a glass gallon jug and add the vodka. Cover tightly and shake well. Allow this liquid to sit for one month. Shake it daily. Strain and filter the liqueur into a clean container and cover it to prevent alcohol evaporation. Boil the water and stir in the sugar to dissolve. When cool, add the sugar syrup to the liqueur. Stir well and then bottle. Use attractive bottles if available. Allow the peach liqueur to age for three months before using.

PLUM LIQUEUR

6 large red plums
2 cups vodka
1 cup sugar
1 cup water

This recipe produces a great tasting plum-flavored liqueur that makes a nice addition to a meal of Oriental food. Begin by carefully inspecting the fruit and washing it if you suspect that it has been sprayed. Gently crush the fruit and place it in a clean gallon glass jug. Pour in the vodka and cover. Boil the water and dissolve the sugar. When this liquid cools, add to the vodka and plums. Cover and let it sit for one month. Agitate daily. Store it in a dark place at room temperature. After one month, strain and filter the liqueur and bottle it. Let it age for at least three months before use.

A good alternative to this recipe and one that tends to be clearer is to use only plum pits rather than the whole fruits. You will need approximately 2 cups of plum pits. They should be scrubbed with a stiff bristled brush to remove the plum meat before use. Follow the same directions as given for the other plum liqueur.

Nonalcoholic Beverages

Once you have developed some brewing skills, you will undoubtedly want to include nonalcoholic drinks that can be enjoyed by all family members. Many nonalcoholic beverages included here were considered medicinal in the United States from approximately 1800 to 1900. They are still used today for medicinal purposes in rural parts of the country, notably the Southeast. The root beer discussed here is said to calm and cleanse the digestive tract.

Nonalcoholic beverages are not allowed to ferment. Much less work is involved in making nonalcoholic beverages. Because many nonalcoholic beverages are bottled as soon as they are mixed, little specialized equipment is needed.

Many soft drinks contain artificial flavors, colorings, chemical additives, and other ingredients over which we have no control. It is possible to produce good tasting soft drinks that do not contain potentially dangerous ingredients. You will also realize a considerable savings over time. Five gallons of root beer can be made at home for about $5.

REGULAR ROOT BEER

This popular drink is very simple to make. Buy one of the many root beer extract syrups on the market. One bottle of root beer extract syrup will produce 5 gallons of root beer. You will also need 4 pounds of white sugar and a package of bakers' yeast.

The best type of bottle for homemade root beer is a high-pressure bottle such as that used for champagne and other highly carbonated beverages. The ingredients for root beer are mixed together, yeast is added, then the liquid is bottled immediately. The root beer is in the bottles before the yeast has started to work fully. The yeast begins to work on the sugar after bottling, resulting in quite a bit of carbon dioxide. Thin-walled bottles simply cannot withstand this internal pressure and should not be used for bottling root beer.

You need a 5-gallon container or canning pot, siphon hose, and enough bottles for the root beer. The bottles must be clean and sterilized thoroughly before use. See Chapter 4.

When all the bottles have been cleaned and sterilized properly, you can begin making root beer. Add the root beer extract syrup to 4 pounds of white sugar and mix thoroughly. Add 4.75 gallons of lukewarm water and stir to completely dissolve the syrup and white sugar. Let this liquid sit undisturbed while you start the yeast culture.

You will also need .5 teaspoon of bakers' yeast (or half a cake of compressed yeast) that has been dissolved in 2 cups of lukewarm water. Stir the yeast into the water. Allow this mixture to sit for about five minutes. After the yeast has begun to work, pour the liquid through cheesecloth into the root beer. The reason for straining the yeast is to remove most of the yeast solids. Stir the strained yeast into the root beer and bottle immediately.

The previously mentioned directions for yeast apply when

making root beer during the warm months. You must add about twice the amount of yeast during colder months.

After the yeast has been stirred into the root beer, bottle as quickly as possible to prevent spoilage from airborne materials. A siphon hose fitted with a special cutoff clip will make the work progress quickly and easily. If you do not have a siphon hose, you will have to use a funnel.

Fill each bottle up to about .5 inch from the top. Wipe the tip of the neck off with a damp cloth and install a crimp cap. After you have several bottles filled, cap them and move them out of the way. Continue in this manner until all the root beer is bottled and capped.

After capping the root beer, store it for at least five days. Place the bottles on their sides in a warm area—ideally between 70 to 80 degrees Fahrenheit. The root beer will have a sour taste if it is stored in a cool area immediately after bottling. Additionally, the root beer will be flat when stored in a cool place. The reason is that the yeast organisms will be killed by the lower temperatures.

After five days, open a bottle of root beer to see if it is ready to drink. You may refrigerate the root beer before trying. The root beer is ready to drink when it is effervescent. This aging may take longer in cooler weather. Root beer made according to these directions will last for about six months. Then it may develop a sour taste. Do not try to store root beer for extended periods.

LOW CALORIE ROOT BEER

If you are concerned about calories, this root beer recipe uses little white sugar. This amount is necessary for the yeast to produce carbon dioxide that carbonates the beverage. You may add a small amount of sugar to sweeten the root beer.

1 bottle of root beer extract
.75 cup (6 ounces) white sugar
1 level teaspoonful bakers' yeast
4.75 gallons water (warmed to 110 degrees Fahrenheit)

Mix the ingredients and bottle according to the instructions for regular root beer. This low calorie root beer is ready to drink after about five days of storage at 70 to 80 degrees Fahrenheit. Small amounts of artificial sweetener may be added before drinking.

SARSAPARILLA

1 pound crushed guaiacum bark
.25 pound guaiacum wood (sawdust)
1 20-gram crushed licorice root
2 ounces aniseed
1.5 ounces mezereon root
1 ounce ground cloves
3.5 pounds white sugar
9 quarts hot water (180 degrees Fahrenheit)

This old recipe results in a medicinal sarsaparilla that is said to calm and cleanse the system when taken three to four times a day in 1-ounce doses.

Mix ingredients together in a nonmetallic container and cover. Let the mixture sit for one week, stirring once a day. The sarsaparilla then is ready for use. It is said to be a blood purifier. Some recipes call for half the amount of sugar given above, substituting 2 cups of dark molasses.

Another recipe uses sarsaparilla extract (which is much easier to find than the ingredients listed earlier). Simply mix one bottle of sarsaparilla extract in 1 pint of hot water. After the mixture cools, add one bottle of pale ale. Allow this mixture to sit undisturbed for two days and then bottle; small bottles are best. This sarsaparilla is ready to use after it has been in the bottle for one week.

SPRUCE BEER

You can make a spruce beer that is a *diuretic* and *antiscorbutic*. Two are given here. A third variation can be made by using fresh spruce bark; approximately .25 pound of fresh material is required.

Recipe One

.5 ounce spruce essence syrup
1 pound white sugar
1 gallon boiling water
1 package bakers' yeast

Boil the water, remove from heat, and add sugar. Stir to dissolve. Add spruce essence syrup and stir. When the mixture cools to about 80 degrees Fahrenheit, add the yeast and stir. Let the liquid sit covered and undisturbed for 24 hours, then bottle and cap. Spruce beer is ready for drinking after it has aged one week. It can be stored for up to two years. Six to 8-ounce bottles are best.

Recipe Two

8 ounces spruce essence
4 ounces crushed ginger
4 ounces hops (pelletized)
3 gallons water
5 pounds white sugar
10 gallons water
2 packages bakers' yeast

Boil 3 gallons of water and add ginger, spruce essence, and

hops. Boil for another 10 minutes and remove from the heat. Add the sugar, stirring to dissolve. Add the hot mixture to 10 gallons of cold water so the resultant mixture is lukewarm. Add yeast and cover. Bottle after 24 to 36 hours, at which time fermentation will have stopped. Cool before serving.

BITTERS

Bitters traditionally were used as stomach calmatives, but their primary use is in flavoring alcoholic drinks. One recipe for bitters calls for 28 different ingredients. The two offered here are quite simple to make.

Recipe One

12 *ounces sliced gentian root*
10 *ounces cinnamon sticks*
10 *ounces caraway seeds*
 2 *ounces juniper berries*
 1 *ounce cloves*
 2 *quarts 100 proof vodka*
2.5 *gallons water*

Mix all ingredients together except the water. Allow the mixture to sit covered and undisturbed for one week. Strain the liquid and add water. Bottle and allow one month for aging before use. These bitters will store well for up to two years.

Recipe Two

2.5 *ounces angostura bark*
1 *ounce gentian root*
.5 *ounce cardamom seeds*
4 *ounces orange peel*
.5 *ounce caraway seeds*

.25 ounce cloves
.5 ounce cinnamon sticks
2 gallons water

Boil the water and stir in all ingredients. Cool, cover, let the mixture sit undisturbed for 24 hours, then bottle. These bitters are ready for use after one month of storage.

APPLE CIDER

Apple cider is a traditional fall drink. Many types are available commercially. Unfortunately, most of the bottled and frozen concentrate apple cider has been heavily processed—chemical preservatives, pasteurized, strained, etc. The result is an apple-flavored beverage that is very clear. If you have access to many fresh apples, you can easily make apple cider that will taste much better than store-bought cider. You can also produce your own vinegar, applejack, and even hard cider.

Many older cider recipes call for using apples that come from natural trees. This means apples from trees that have not been sprayed and are really not suitable for eating out of hand. In most areas of the country these apple trees exist, especially around deserted homesteads and farms. These apples are commonly unattractive compared to those found in supermarkets. Many people feel that the juice from these apples is far superior to any other available.

Making apple cider is not difficult, especially if the beverage is made and drank within a few days. More work is involved if you want to store the beverage for extended periods or to make other apple-based beverages.

The only piece of specialized equipment you need is a cider or fruit press. Some presses come fully assembled, and others are in kit form.

You can rent a cider press from your local beer and wine making supply store. A grape press is suitable for squeezing apples. Make sure that you rent a large-capacity press, and the squeezing will go quickly and smoothly.

You can expect to produce about 3 gallons of fresh cider from each bushel of apples. Almost any type of apples will do. Sort through the apples before squeezing and remove any that are infested with insects or rotten. Apples can be cut up to remove damaged areas before squeezing, but this operation will require much more time. Get some help when squeezing apples.

Wash the apples in water before using them. Allow the apples to air dry before squeezing, or your sweet cider will be diluted with wash water.

After the apples have been cleaned and inspected, you can begin squeezing the cider. You will need clean containers. Allow approximately 3 gallons of cider per bushel. Clean and sterilize all containers.

Filter the cider before bottling to remove impurities and solid matter. Cheesecloth stretched over a large funnel makes filtering fairly simple. Use enough layers of cheesecloth to give the desired filtering effect. Replace the cheesecloth often as it tends to clog with sediment and other material from the cider.

The procedure for squeezing the apples depends on the type of press you are using. If you rented a grape press, simply fill up the bin and screw down the compression ram. If you are using another type of press, you may have to wrap the apples in bundles of burlap or other suitable material before crushing.

Apply pressure slowly and gradually for best results. If you try to extract cider by applying too much pressure too quickly, the cider will be cloudy. You also run the risk of bursting the fabric, assuming the apples were wrapped first before squeezing.

The proper way to squeeze apples is to turn the ram screw once and wait a few moments. Juice will begin to flow almost as soon as pressure is applied. After about one minute, increase the pressure on the ram by turning the screw one full revolution. Stop and allow the juice to run off. Slow and gradual pressure will produce the best looking and tasting cider.

When you reach the point where a turn of the screw produces little cider or apple juice, clean out the press and start over again. The apple pomace should be removed from the press before adding new apples to be squeezed. Wash off the press with water from a garden hose.

You can drink cider as soon as it comes out of the press—after filtering. Fresh cider will keep for about two weeks in a sealed container in your refrigerator. The cider tends to become cloudy and slightly sour beyond this period.

Fresh apple cider can be stored in your freezer for up to one year. Simply fill plastic containers such as gallon milk jugs and place them in a chest-type freezer. Fill containers only about 90 percent full to reduce the possibility of them bursting when the cider freezes.

You can also store fresh cider for long periods by first pasteurizing it. Simply heat the cider up to 170 degrees Fahrenheit and hold this temperature for about 10 minutes. Bottle and seal with crown caps. Bottles must be sterilized first to ensure that there are no contaminants inside. Once apple cider has been pasteurized, it is then rightfully considered apple juice rather than cider. Apple juice can be stored almost indefinitely.

Chemical additives can also be used to prolong the storage life of apple cider and juice. Add 1 ounce of potassium sorbate to every 2 gallons of cider before bottling. Make certain that the potassium sorbate is completely dissolved by stirring. Cider with potassium sorbate added will keep well for several weeks in the refrigerator, and you will probably not notice the addition of the chemical preservative.

Hard Cider

Hard cider is very simple to make, but the fermentation process takes about one year for best results. Begin by filling a fermentation vessel—1 to 5-gallon size—with fresh cider. Add 1 cup of dried raisins per gallon of cider. Fit the fermentation vessel with an air lock and let it sit undisturbed until all activity ceases. In most cases this will take about one month. Siphon off the cider and bottle in clean, sterilized containers; capped bottles work fine. Store the beverage for about one year, then drink. The containers must be sealed well, or the hard cider will turn to vinegar. Some people like to add a stick or two of cinnamon, cloves, ginger, or other spices along with the raisins for added flavor.

Applejack

Applejack is an alcoholic beverage made from hard cider. Make hard cider as discussed earlier. After the liquid has been in bottles for one year, place them in an area where they will partially freeze. Alcohol does not freeze, but apple cider does. Simply pour off the applejack after one day of freezing. Applejack is a powerful drink that should not be taken lightly. The traditional way of making applejack is to use wooden barrels. After two years of storage, the barrels are rolled out into a snowbank and allowed to partially freeze. The real applejack is poured off.

Apple Mead

Apple mead is another beverage that can easily be made from fresh apple cider. This is a special drink that is suitable for festive occasions such as Thanksgiving and Christmas. If made in the fall, this great tasting beverage will be ready for the holidays. Mix equal amounts of fresh apple cider and honey. Stir the liquid to completely dissolve the honey. Place it in a stone crock or gall container and cover. Allow the liquid to sit undisturbed for several weeks until all activity ceases. Then skim off the top foam and bottle.

Cider Vinegar

Cider vinegar is very useful when making pickles, relish, and some German meat dishes. It is very easy to make if you have a ready supply of apples. Cider vinegar contains a corrosive acid. When working with this liquid, do not use copper, zinc, iron, or galvanized containers. The interaction of this acid and these metals will produce a deadly poison.

The easiest way to make apple cider vinegar is to place a few gallons of fresh apple cider in an open nonmetallic container and cover with a cloth. The liquid will turn to vinegar within a few days, and a foam "mother" culture will form on top. Skim this material off, and the cider vinegar is ready for use. It can be bottled or simply put in screw-top bottles until needed.

An alternate method of making cider vinegar involves adding .25 pound of white sugar to every quart of fresh apple cider. Stir to dissolve, then add one-quarter package of dried bakers' yeast to every gallon of the liquid. Let it sit undisturbed for several weeks or until all yeast activity ceases. The container should be covered with a cloth during this period. After fermentation ceases, siphon off the vinegar and bottle. You may want to add herbs like tarragon, basil, and oregano to make special salad dressing vinegar.

GRAPE JUICE

Grape juice is another fruit drink that is very simple to make if you have access to a good supply of grapes and a press. You might also want to try your hand at wine making. All the steps in making grape juice are identical to those used in the preliminary stages of wine making.

Probably the most common grape in the United States is the *concord*. The juice from this grape makes an ideal beverage that can be drank immediately or canned or frozen for later use.

Wash and inspect your grapes. Remove and discard all stems, leaves, and other material. Remove any damaged or rotten grapes, too.

Place the clean grapes in a press and slowly extract the juice. Before putting the juice in clean containers, let it sit undisturbed for several hours so that the tannin settles to the bottom. Slowly pour off the juice and filter through cheesecloth. The fresh grape juice is ready for drinking immediately, or it can be stored by canning or freezing.

To can grape juice, you will need standard quart canning jars with screw-type canning lids and a canning pot full of boiling water. Place the fresh grape juice in an enamel pot and heat to 170 degrees Fahrenheit. Hold this temperature for 10 minutes. Pour the juice into sterilized canning jars. Screw down the lids and place the jars in a hot water bath. Boil for 30 minutes and then remove the jars. Cool and place in storage. Grape juice canned in this manner will last for two years. The grape juice can also be used to make grape jelly.

If you have a large freezer, the easiest way to save grape juice is to freeze it in plastic containers until ready to use. After squeezing the grape juice place the liquid in quart or gallon-size plastic jugs. Fill each container only to about 90 percent of capacity so the freezing juice will have some expanding room. Place them in your freezer. When thawed, frozen grape juice makes a great drink and can also be used for making grape jelly.

Problems and Solutions

You must provide a sterile atmosphere for fermentation when brewing beer. Cooking pots, primary and secondary fermenters, siphon hose, and beer bottles must be treated before use to kill any bacteria or other harmful microorganisms that may be present. If you carefully follow the instructions for sterilization and accepted brewing techniques outlined earlier, you will greatly reduce the chances of failure. Nevertheless, problems sometimes occur. This chapter covers the most common problems in the home brewery.

TEMPERATURE

The range of acceptable temperatures for mashing is from 110 to 160 degrees Fahrenheit. The mash will be damaged by temperatures of more than 170 degrees Fahrenheit. While fermentation can be accelerated by a temperature of 70 degrees Fahrenheit, it is far better to ferment at 50 degrees Fahrenheit. The best temperature for aging most beers, ales, and stouts is from 50 to 65 degrees Fahrenheit. Even the temperature of the brew before serving can affect the taste, clarity, and overall condition of the beer. Almost all the recipes given previously offer suggestions for serving temperatures. People in the major beer drinking countries drink beer, ale, and stout at room temperature, we Americans tend to chill our beers to 35 degrees Fahrenheit. Commercial brewers put special additives in their beers to prevent problems when the beer is chilled this low.

CIDERY TASTE

The most common cause of a *cidery taste* in home brewed beer is using white cane sugar. Cane sugar is not as fermentable as corn sugar. The home brew thus resembles cider more than beer. Some home brewers prefer the cidery taste.

CLOUDINESS

Cloudiness in home brewed beer is much more of a problem in pale or clear beers than in amber or dark beers, simply because we are used to thinking of beer as being crystal clear. Commercial brewers achieve a clear product through various methods of filtration and chemical additives. Because we want to avoid additives whenever possible, we must resort to other measures.

Probably the greatest cause of cloudiness in home brew is not decanting the beer properly. Every bottle of home brew will contain a bit of yeast sediment in the bottom. Before serving, the beer should be carefully decanted into a clean container. Leave the sediment in the bottle. If the bottle is shook before decanting, the yeast sediment will be dispersed throughout the liquid and will form a cloudy haze in the beer. Store the beer undisturbed. Chill and decant carefully, and your beer will be very clear.

Other causes of haze in home brewed beer include insufficient mashing of crushed malted barley (starch may still be present) and the so-called "chill haze" that only appears after the beer has been refrigerated. The only solution to a starch haze in beer is to continue mashing until the iodine starch test reveals that no starches are present.

Sometimes the only solution to a chill haze problem is to drink your beer out of a ceramic mug or tankard rather than a clear glass. Several powders can be added to the beer before bottling to solve a haze problem. Isinglass, gypsum, and other finings are available.

Another solution to a haze problem is to allow your beer to sit for a longer period in the secondary fermenter before bottling. This will naturally cause more sedimentation and, as a rule, clearer beer. When transferring the contents of the secondary fermenter into a 5-gallon container for bulk priming and bottling, siphon very carefully so as not to disturb the sediment in the bottom of the fermenter.

EXPLOSIONS

The most common cause of exploding bottled beer is bottling before the beer is fully fermented. Take a hydrometer reading for several days prior to bottling. Do not bottle until the reading remains constant for two or three days. Another cause of explosions is too much priming sugar. Use only the amount of sugar recommended in the recipe. Bulk priming is usually a better technique than priming individual bottles.

FLAT BEER

Flat beer is most commonly caused by poor or improper conditioning. Other causes include inadequate priming prior to bottling and poor quality caps that allow carbon dioxide to escape rather than being absorbed into the beer. As a rule, do not drink any beer until it has aged for a minimum of two weeks. The beer generally will be better after it has aged for at least six weeks. Prime with the recommended amount of corn sugar. If all else fails, check the condition of the caps you are using. Often cork-lined caps do not seal well. Plastic-lined crown caps soaked in warm water before use are the best choice for a good seal. The caps should be crimped fully.

HEAD QUALITY

Beers brewed with malt extract syrup tend to have poorer quality heads than beers made with whole grains. Nevertheless, a good head is possible with the former. If you find that your beer either lacks a head or has a head of poor quality, let the beer age for a longer period before serving. Two to three months will help the beer develop a good head. Decant the beer prior to serving in a glass or mug. Before decanting or pouring, however, rinse the container and glass in clear water. Glasses washed in detergent that may remain on the surface will prevent a good head from forming.

INFECTION

Infection may result in a sour aroma, off-color and, in an extreme case, in a gelatinous glob in the beer bottle. Infection is most commonly caused by improper sanitation. Follow the suggestions given in Chapter 2 for cleaning equipment and bottles.

Another source of infection is a slow-acting yeast. If the yeast does not work well, carbon dioxide, which forms a shield over the brew in the primary fermenter, is nonexistent. The beer in the primary fermenter should be vigorously active within a few hours of pitching in the brewer's yeast. If this is not the case, add a yeast nutrient.

If you discover that a batch of beer has been infected, the only thing you can do is to dump it. Sterilize all equipment and bottles in a bleach solution.

SLOW FERMENTATION

Fermentation should be evident by vigorous activity initially in the primary fermenter, then again in the secondary fermenter. In addition to a poor quality yeast, cold temperatures will often slow fermentation. As long as the beer is protected from the surrounding atmosphere by being in a fermenter fitted with an air lock, there is little cause for alarm. Use your hydrometer several times during fermentation to help in determining when fermentation is complete. The most ideal temperature range for fermentation at the home brewing level is from 50 to 65 degrees Fahrenheit. Higher temperatures tend to make the beer ferment too vigorously.

YEAST BITE OR FLAVOR

A beer with a heavy yeast flavor is not very pleasant to drink, even though the excess yeast will not harm you. To avoid this problem, use only brewer's yeast—either top or bottom-fermenting types—in standard amounts. Before transferring the contents of the primary fermenter to the secondary fermenter, many brewers like to skim the foam and residue that forms on top. If this does not cure the problem, let your beer sit in the secondary fermenter for longer periods. Make certain that the fermenter is fitted with a good air lock to exclude the atmosphere.

TASTE

Taste is really a personal matter. Nevertheless, certain guidelines can be used for judging the taste of a beer, ale, or stout. Pale beers generally should be lightly hopped and dry. Darker beers should be slightly heavier hopped and be a bit sweeter, but generally they have more body. Ales tend to be heavily hopped, more robust in flavor, and have a higher alcoholic content. Stouts are very heavy and dark. They should be heavily hopped, but they can range from dry to an almost syrupy sweetness. If the beer tastes good, drink it. If it doesn't takes very good, drink it anyway and try to correct the taste in the next batch you make.

Appendix

Suppliers

The following companies offer beer and wine making supplies and materials through mail order. All have catalogs. Prices vary. Some companies pay postage on all items; others do not. Shop wisely and you can save plenty of money.

Bet-Mar
2602D Devine
Columbia, SC 29205

Cask & Keg
Dept. 53, Box 12A Rt. 1
Mattawan, MI 49071

Continental
P.O. Box 68016
Indianapolis, IN 46268

Gourmet
5133-N Fairhill
Philadelphia, PA 19120

Great Fermentations
87M Larkspur
San Rafael, CA 94901

Kraus
P.O. Box 7850
Independence, MO 64053

Semplex
Box 12276 K
Minneapolis, MN 55412

S.P.I.
P.O. Box 784-E
Chapel Hill, NC 27514

Vynox
Box A 7498
Rochester, NY 14615

Wine Hobby
P.O. Box G 104
Greenwood, MA 01880

Wine Works
5175-A West Alameda
Denver, CO 80219

Glossary

acetic acid—The colorless, acidic liquid found in vinegar. This acid can also develop by exposing the wort to the atmosphere.

adjuncts—Grains other than barley that are used to supply starches in brewing. Adjuncts are most commonly used in conjunction with barley, and they are very common in American brewing. Corn, rice, and wheat are the major malt adjuncts.

air lock—A device used as a one-way cap during fermentation. Pressure from the fermenter is allowed to escape through water while the atmosphere is excluded.

alcohol—A colorless volatile liquid produced through the natural process of yeast organisms eating starches, which are converted into fermentable sugars.

ale—Generic term for British-style, top-fermented beer. Most ales are copper-colored, but some are much darker though clear.

antioxidant—Added to beer at bottling time to prevent harmful oxidation. Ascorbic acid is most commonly added prior to bottling.

aroma—The pleasing smell of beer that is derived mainly from the hops used.

arrack—A spirit distilled from rum.

attenuation—The lowering of the specific gravity of the wort by the natural production of alcohol.

autolysis—The decomposition of dead yeast cells that releases nitrogen used by living organisms. Nitrogen also produces an off taste in the beer so it is necessary to rack the beer several times before bottling.

barley corn—Whole barley grain used in the brewing of beer.

barrel—The standard measure of beer equal to about 31.5 gallons in the United States and 36 imperial gallons in Great Britain.

bitters—Stout that is top-fermented, dark in color, and bitter.

bock—A dark beer that is only produced during the zodiac period of Capricorn (December 22 through January 20).

body—A term used to describe the lightness or heaviness of a beer. Heavy beers generally have more body than light beers.

brewmaster—The person who takes full responsibility for brewing.

calcium sulfate—Additive for lowering the pH of water used in mashing barley malt. It is found in Burton water salts.

caramel—When sugar is heated, it will darken and turn into caramel. It is used for coloring dark beers and stouts.

carbon dioxide—An inert gas produced during fermentation.

carrageen moss—Sometimes called Irish moss, it is added to boiling wort to assist in the clarification of finished beer.

caudle—A warm drink that is said to be good for sick persons—especially a mixture of ale with eggs, bread, sugar, and spices.

cidery—A common flavor of home brew caused by using white sugar. The taste is much like cider which many people find enjoyable.

conditioning—Allowing beer to "sleep" for at least six weeks during which time it will clear and carbonate itself by producing carbon dioxide.

cutting—Adding water to wort before primary fermentation begins. Also, arresting fermentation by adding clarifiers such as gypsum or finings.

dextrins—Gummy polysaccharides produced during the mashing process of malt. Dextrins are not fermentable, but they contribute to the terminal gravity and body of the brew.

dextrose—Corn sugar—the most fermentable sugar for brewing beer.

diastase—Amylase enzymes that can be added to the mash to accent the conversion of starches into fermentable sugars.

dram—A small drink of alcohol equal to .0625 ounce.

draught—British spelling of draft. It means to draw from a keg or barrel.

elixir—A sweetened liquid usually containing alcohol that is used as a vehicle for medicinal agents.

extract—The liquid derived from mashing malted barley (and commercially malt adjuncts).

fermentation—The production of alcohol as a result of the actions of yeast organisms on sugar.

fermentation lock—See *air lock*.

finings—The substances used for clearing beer such as isinglass, gypsum, gelatin, etc.

flakes—Flaked corn or rice added to mash by many commercial brewers to derive an inexpensive source of fermentable sugars. Flaked corn will give a dry taste to ale.

flip—A spiced, sweetened drink of ale or beer to which a beaten egg has been added.

gill—A British measurement of 4 ounces.

grist—The dry mixture of barley malt and malt adjuncts prior to mashing.

head—In brewing, the white foam that forms on top of beer when the liquid is poured into a glass. The dextrins in the wort are responsible for the head. Store the beer at least six weeks after bottling to help it develop a good head.

heading liquid—An additive that will increase head quality and retention, assuming that all other requirements are followed.

home brew—A fermentation of malt, sugar, hops, water, and yeast that is not made commercially.

hop oil—A concentrate of the oils in many hop plants. It is used primarily in commercial brewing to the rate of about four drops per barrel.

hops—The dried blossom of the female hop plant that is boiled in the wort to extract flavors and aroma. Hops are among the fastest growing plants on earth and help to preserve beer.

hydrometer—An instrument used for measuring the specific gravity of a liquid.

initial heat—The temperature of the liquor immediately after mixing malt and hot water; the temperature of the wort when beginning.

invert sugar—Sugar that has been treated with a low acid solution. This sugar starts fermenting more quickly than cane sugars.

isinglass—A powder made from the bladder of the sturgeon which, when mixed into fermented beer, will have a clearing effect.

krausening—The addition of strong newly fermenting wort to produce natural carbonation.

lactose—Sugar that is derived from milk and cannot be fermented by yeasts. It is most commonly added to stout as a sweetener—thus the term milk stout.

lager—A generic term describing any bottom-fermented (yeast-type) beer. All bottom-fermented beers are lagers.

lees—Dead yeast cultures that collect in the bottom of a fermentation vessel and bottles.

liquor—An alcoholic beverage that is usually distilled rather than fermented.

malt—Malted barley; barley grain that has been germinated. The three main types used in brewing (in order of popularity) are pale, crystal, and black.

malt adjuncts—Other grains (corn, rice, and wheat) that are used to produce fermentable sugars in conjunction with malted barley.

malt extract—A syrup that is obtained by mashing malted barley.

maltose—The sugar derived from mashing malted barley.

mashing—The cooking at specific temperatures of malted barley to produce a malt extract.

mash tun—The pot used for cooking malted barley during the mashing process.

nectar—A sweet liquid secreted from the nectaries of a plant; a drink of the gods.

nutrients—Sources of necessary elements (phosphorus,

nitrogen, etc.) that are required for keeping yeast cultures healthy during fermentation.

pasteurization—The heating of beer commercially in the bottle or can to stabilize the beer. This is generally not done in European countries (except exported beers), but it is done to most American beers (except keg beers).

perry—A fermented drink made from pears.

pH—The accepted expression of the acidity of a liquid. Range is from highly acidic, 0.0, to neutral, 7.0, to highly alkaline, 14.0.

pilsner—The world's most popular beer. It is pale in color, well hopped, and is not made in this country commercially very much.

pitching temperature—The temperature of the wort when the yeast is added—ideally, 60 degrees Fahrenheit.

pop—A beverage consisting of soda water, flavoring, and a sweet syrup.

porter—A weak stout that is rich in saccharine matter and contains about 4 percent alcohol.

posset—Hot sweetened and spiced milk that has been curdled with ale or beer; it has medicinal qualities.

primary fermenter—A large vessel used for the first stage of fermentation.

priming—The addition of corn sugar just prior to bottling. This sugar causes a slight additional fermentation and carbonation in beer.

racking—Removing the beer from the lees by siphoning.

ratafia—Any liqueur flavored with fruit kernels and bitter almonds.

rousing—The vigorous stirring of beer to assist and encourage fermentation.

running—Refers to the wort as it is drawn off the mash tun.

secondary fermenter—A vessel used for the second phase of fermentation to which an air lock has been attached.

single stage fermenter—A vessel in which both primary and secondary fermentation occur and to which a special fermentation lock has been fitted.

siphon—Transferring the contents of one container to another through a hose.

skimming—Removing the foam that forms on the wort during primary fermentation.

sour—The deterioration of beer as a result of either being exposed to the atmosphere or unsanitary conditions in the brewery.

sparging—The washing or rinsing of grains used in the mashing process to recover as much fermentable sugars and dextrins as possible for the wort.

specific gravity—The density of a liquid as compared with that of water (which is 1.000). This measurement is taken with a hydrometer.

starting gravity—The specific gravity of the wort prior to fermentation.

steam beer—American beer made with bottom-fermenting yeast and at a temperature of between 60 to 70 degrees Fahrenheit.

sterilize—To free from living microorganisms either through heat or chemical action.

stout—A dark, heavily hopped, bittersweet beer that has been fermented with a top-fermenting yeast.

striking temperature—The temperature at which the mashing grain (barley malt) is introduced to the liquor.

stuck fermentation—The stoppage of fermentation before terminal gravity has been reached. The most common causes are poor quality yeast cultures and/or low temperatures.

sucrose—White table sugar that comes from cane. This sugar is not recommended for brewing beer because it is not readily fermentable.

sulfite—Sodium metabisulfite or sodium bisulfite that produces carbon dioxide when mixed with water. It is most commonly used as a sterilizing agent.

tankard—A tall, one-handed drinking vessel most commonly made from pewter or ceramic.

terminal gravity—The specific gravity of the beer when fermentation is complete; the time to bottle beer; when all fermentable sugars have been fermented and converted to alcohol and carbon dioxide.

turbid—A cloudy quality in beer.

water treatment—The increase of the overall pH of water used in mashing barley malt.

wheat beer—Beer made with the addition of wheat grain.

wort—The crushed malted grains are mixed with liquor at a predetermined temperature until the starch in the grains is converted into fermentable sugars by the action of diastase. This liquid is called the wort.

yeast—A yellowish surface froth or sediment that occurs especially in saccharine liquids (as fruit juices) in which it promotes alcoholic fermentation. Bottom-fermenting yeast is used for lager beers. Top-fermenting yeast is used mainly for ales.

Index

Lowenbrau, 3
Lowenbrau style beer recipe, 125

M

Malt, 55, 60, 189
Malt, black, 61
Malt, crystal, 61
Malt, fully modified, 61
Malt, pale, 60
Malt, undermodified, 61
Malt extract, 57
Malt extract syrup, bulk, 59
Malt extract syrups, 58
Malt extract syrups, Blue Ribbon, 58
Malt extract syrups, John Bull, 58
Malt extract syrups, Munton & Fison, 58
Malt extract syrups, Superbrau, 58
Maltose, 73, 189
Mashing, 7, 189
Mashing grains, 104
Mashing off, 57
Mash tun, 39, 189
Meat grinder, 106
Medicinal stout recipe, 154
Meniscus effect, 43
Mezereon root, 168
Mild light grain beer recipe, 133
Mild stout recipe, 153
Miller, 5
Miller High Life, 3
Mint, 66
Molson, 3
Moose Head Ale, 3
Munchner, 3
Munton & Fison malt extract syrups, 58
Murphy's ale recipe, 148

N

Nectar, 189
Nonalcoholic beverages, 165
Northern European style beer recipe, 136
Nutrients, 189

O

Oats, 63
Olympia, 3
Orange liqueur recipe, 162
Oregano, 175
Origins of beer, 1

P

Pale ale recipe, 141
Pale American beer recipe, 134

Pale European style beer recipe, 126
Pale malt, 59
Pasteur, Louis, 1
Pasteurization, 1, 190
Peach liqueur recipe, 162
Pennyroyal, 66
Perry, 190
pH, 52
pH of water, 104
Pilsner, 3
Pitching temperature, 190
Plum liqueur recipe, 163
Polysaccharides, /
Pop, 190
Porter, 4, 190
Porter recipe, 130
Posset, 190
Potassium sorbate, 174
Pot for boiling, 19
Primary fermenter, 9, 18
Priming, 190
Priming beer, 99
Problems in brewing, 177
Proteases, 12
Proteinase, 60

R

Racking, 191
Rainer Ale, 3
Ratafia, 191
Real man's stout recipe, 151
Recipe, amber ale made from extract, 142
Recipe, amber all-grain beer, 132
Recipe, amber European style beer, 123
Recipe, apricot liqueur, 157
Recipe, Australian all-grain beer, 138
Recipe, Australian sundowner's ale, 147
Recipe, basic beer, 119
Recipe, blueberry liqueur, 158
Recipe, buccaneer stout, 152
Recipe, Canadian Molsonlike beer, 129
Recipe, chamomile liqueur, 159
Recipe, cherry liqueur, 159
Recipe, coffee liqueur, 160
Recipe, dark European style beer, 122
Recipe, dark European style grain beer, 131
Recipe, dark heavy-hopped European beer, 135
Recipe, dark pilsner number one, 139
Recipe, dark pilsner number two, 139